CU00336475

ADVISORY
EXPLICIT CONTENT

ADVANCED SWEARING HANDBOOK

MARK LEIGH & MIKE LEPINE

summersdale

ADVANCED SWEARING HANDBOOK

Copyright © Summersdale Publishers Ltd 2005

Text by Iliterati International

The right of Mark Leigh and Mike Lepine to be identified as
the authors of this work has been asserted in accordance
with sections 77 and 78 of the Copyright, Designs and
Patents Act 1988.

Summersdale Publishers Ltd
46 West Street
Chichester
West Sussex
PO19 1RP
UK

www.summersdale.com

Printed and bound in Great Britain

ISBN 1 84024 477 1

Important

Please note: this book is full of words like fuck, shit, cocksucker, piss, motherfucker and cunt, so if you're at all offended by bad language it's too late now and you might as well read on.

About The Authors

Mike Lepine

Mike Lepine encourages completely free speech in his household. Sometimes this means far-ranging discussions on the implications posed by the paired connectivity of widely separated subatomic particles for faster-than-light travel. More often though, it just means swearing at the TV news and his impressionable young son telling Tigger to 'fuck off!' at Eurodisney.

Mike's loudest, most inventive and most prolonged bout of swearing came last year when he encountered George Galloway's Respect Party battle bus outside Leicester Station.

Mark Leigh

Mark is no stranger to swearing, as he is constantly being told to 'fuck off' by his work colleagues, clients, friends, relatives, neighbours, random strangers and his parents.

He thinks English is the best language in the whole wide world because, as he says, 'the fucking Eskimos might have seventeen different words for "snow" but we have fifty-eight words for the vagina, many of them quite rude.'

Mark's ambition is to make love to Hollywood actress Scarlett Johannson (or better still, fuck her).

Thank you...

Mike Lepine would like to thank Ashwin Bedi, Anju Dutta, Gage Hatton-Lepine, Philippa Hatton-Lepine and Colin Higgs for their patience and/or assistance.

Mark Leigh got absolutely no fucking help from anyone and if his so-called 'friends' are reading this, they can all piss off.

Introduction

When angry, count to four;
when very angry, swear

Mark Twain

It's a fair guess that swearing has been around as long as human speech. Although there are no written records, you can be sure that any caveman who had just stubbed his toe on a stalagmite or was annoyed by his wife serving up mammoth broth yet again had a few choice cuss words on hand to express his displeasure.

And just as we have evolved, so has our swearing. When we were a more religious people, our more serious obscenities were blasphemies. 'Zounds', for example, was a shortening of 'Christ's Wounds' and 'Bloody' was an abbreviation of 'Blood of Mary'. Then, as religious fears were replaced by neuroses about our own sexuality, the swear words of choice started to refer to sex acts and parts of the body.

Today, in our politically-correct times, the real shocking obscenities in our vocabulary – the real taboo words – tend to be those that belittle people of alternative gender, sexuality, race or religion. Once terrifying words like fuck are now the stuff of routine kindergarten conversation.

This is a bit of a pity, as the really choice obscenities of today are nowhere near as versatile and as easily used as we could wish. For example, calling Michael Winner 'a fucking lesbo' makes no sense. It is so unsatisfying. Equally, it is hardly rewarding to call Gordon Brown a 'fat dago poofta' (the correct technical term is fat bastard thieving Scots git).

This is why we should be so grateful for the 'C word' – or cunt. Because it is seen as demeaning to women, it has gained an even greater power to shock while other sexual words have diminished. Cunt is a word we should truly treasure, because it can be so widely applied to anything from your boss to the board members of Central Trains – with real force and impact.

But beware – even cunt is losing its punch. Forty years ago, a book that dared to use the word was the subject of a major British court case. Today, you can pick up this book (which uses the word cunt with gay abandon) from right beside the till, at child's-eye level.

We swear because we are angry. If we have no truly effective swear words left, maybe only violence will suffice...

Mike Lepine & Mark Leigh

11 of the Most Offensive Song Titles

'Cocksucker Blues'

by the Rolling Stones

– written by Mick Jagger to fulfil a contractual agreement; Decca, not surprisingly, refused to release it

'Yo Sister Sucked My Dick'

by Bell Labs Sound

– their lead singer went by the name of 'Ridiculous Rick With The Big Fucking Dick'

'Fist Fucking Baby'

by The Bomb Party

– taking their name from the title of a Graeme Greene novel, the group did not become a commercial success

'Fuck A Dog'

by Blink 182

– singer's lament about not being able to fuck his mum or dad in the arse, so he goes for the dog. Nice

'Slob On My Knob'

by Michael 'Boogaloo' Boyer

– the singer was a DJ in the Memphis Hard Rock Café (with that song title his customers were lucky he wasn't a chef there...)

'Fucked With A Knife'

by Cannibal Corpse

– New York death metal band known for their songs about violent sexual scenarios. Like being fucked with a knife, for example

'Cum Stains On My Pillow'

by David Allen Coe

– sent to reform school aged nine and in and out of correctional facilities until he was 30, Coe is one of the few X-rated country singers

'Moist Vagina'

by Nirvana

– with a song like this who are we to criticise the artistry of Kurt Cobain?

'She Loves My Cock'

by Jackyl

– the chorus consists of the song's title being repeated over and over and over and over. And over

'All Hotties Eat The Jizz'

by Necro

– one of the album covers from this Brooklyn rapper showed a girl sucking on a vibrator that was protruding from the barrel of a gun

'Oh My Pregnant Head (Labia in the Sunlight)'

by The Flaming Lips

– one of the very few songs with the word 'labia' in the title

Male Pet Names for the Female Sex Organ

A recent American survey reported that the top 10 pet names used by men to describe the vagina were:

1. Pussy
2. Cunt
3. Vag
4. Twat

5.Bush
6.Honey-pot
7.Lips
8.Muffy
9.Rose-bud
10.Snatch

Other pet names mentioned (but not ranked) in the survey included: furburger, box, flaps, cave, cunnie, fanny, honey-pie, jelly-cave, sugarbush, love-box, ying-yang, money-pit, tunnel of love, nether lips and pencil sharpener.

2004: A Vintage Year for Rude Names in Academia

In 2004, the University of New York State's Mathematics Department boasted a woman professor by the name of **Sho-Ya Wang**.

The Harvard Clinical Research Institute employed **Richard Kuntz, MD, M.Sc**. as Chief Scientific Officer. Ironically, his speciality was gynaecology.

The Max Planck Institute for Molecular Genetics in Berlin, Germany, boasted an **Erich E. Wanker, Ph.D.**

The University of Maryland employed a **Professor André L. Tits**, while the Universidade de Brasília employed in its Geology Department one **Professor Reinhardt Adolfo Fuck**. (No getting his rocks off jokes required.)

Larry Bumpass was Professor Emeritus of Sociology at the University of Wisconsin-Madison while the Affiliate Professor in the Department of Clinical and Experimental Pharmacology at the University of Adelaide was **Professor Richard Head B.Sc., PhD**.

But first prize has to go to an associate professor at Singapore's National Institute of Education. Her name – **Chew Shit Fun**.

Bogus Priest Busted!

'Fucking Hell' and 'Oh Jesus fucking Christ!' are not words you'd normally associate with the priesthood but exclamations like this alerted Sardinian priest Father Umberto Derium to the possibility that his new cleric, Claudio Goglio, might be an imposter.

Despite Goglio's apparent proficiency in church matters, Father Derium grew suspicious of the profaning priest due to his 'uncharacteristic and colourful language' adding, 'I was suspicious of him right from the start, especially because he kept swearing and blaspheming – something no real priest would ever dream of doing.'

He said, 'For six months he tricked the people by saying Mass and even hearing confessions, when he wasn't even a qualified priest.'

Goglio, 36, whose charade included performing funerals, baptisms and weddings had also managed to dupe the unsuspecting local Archbishop of Alghero into celebrating services with him.

In 2004 Goglio was jailed for a year and fined the equivalent of £400 for masquerading as a priest. The court in the Sardinian town of Olbia also heard evidence that he had stolen money raised in collections.

In his defence, Goglio said he was on a spiritual mission from God, adding, 'I just wanted to help spread the word.'

(It is not clear if he meant the 'F word'.)

Real Place Names Worth a Quick Snigger

ARSOLI
Italy

ARSY
France

BALD KNOB
USA

BASTARDO
Italy

BEAVER
USA

BIG BONE LICK
USA

BLUEBALLS
USA

BRA
Italy

BROWN WILLY
England

CAPE CIRCUMCISION
Bouvet Island

CHINAMAN'S KNOB
Australia

CLIMAX
USA

CLIT
Romania

CRAPOLLA
Italy

CUNTER
Switzerland

(One wonders what the official term is for
people who originate from Cunter...)

CUNTIS
Spain

FELCH
USA

(You may have to be gay to get this one.)

FUKU
China

GAY HEAD
USA

(Apparently the town recently decided to
rename itself Aquinnah. Shame.)

INTERCOURSE
USA

KNOB LICK
USA

LARGO LABIA
Italy

LICKEY END
England

MIDDELFART
Denmark

MIDDLE SPUNK LAKE
USA

MUFF
Northern Ireland

NOBBER
Republic of Ireland

PENISTONE
England

PIS PIS RIVER
Nicaragua

PUSSY
France

RECTUM
Holland

SEMEN
Indonesia

SEXMOAN
The Philippines

SHAFTER
USA

SHAG HARBOUR
Canada

SHITAGOO LAKE
Canada

SOUTH DILDO
Canada

SPUNK CREEK
USA

TE UREWERA NATIONAL PARK
New Zealand

(Hilarious if you're Maori, apparently, as Te Urewera is Maori for 'the burnt penis'.)

TITTYBONG
Australia

TITZ
Germany

TWATT
Scotland

(There's a Twatt on both the Orkneys and
Shetlands, apparently.)

WANG-LIK
China

WANKDORF
Switzerland

WANKER'S CORNER
USA

WANKHAM
Austria

WETWANG
England

The 15 Worst Swear Words

In 1997, the BBC, the Independent Television Commission and the Advertising Standards Association jointly commissioned research into the severity of swear words as perceived by the British public. When they conducted another survey only three years later, they were surprised to see that the results had changed. The results, with the harshest word first, are as follows (the rankings in brackets signify the results from 1997):

2000		1997
1st	Cunt	(1st)
2nd	Motherfucker	(2nd)
3rd	Fuck	(3rd)
4th	Wanker	(4th)
5th	Nigger	(11th)
6th	Bastard	(5th)
7th	Prick	(7th)
8th	Bollocks	(6th)
9th	Arsehole	(9th)
10th	Paki	(17th)
11th	Shag	(8th)
12th	Whore	(13th)
13th	Twat	(10th)
14th	Piss Off	(12th)
15th	Spastic	(14th)

Class and Swearing

One of the lesser-known works of Robert Graves, the celebrated poet and author of *I Claudius*, is *Lars Porsena, or The Future of Swearing and Improper Language*.

Writing in the 1920s, he detected distinct class differences in swear words. Bastard, he said, was a truly grave insult amongst the working classes – where it was far more likely to be true. Amongst the ruling classes, calling someone a bugger was extremely insulting because given the number of practicing homosexuals in the aristocracy it was also likely to be true.

Streets of Shame

In medieval times, the streets around brothels often acquired descriptive names – names which were later changed to protect delicate sensibilities. In fourteenth-century London you could find yourself walking down Slut's Lane or Codpiece Alley (now known as Coppice Alley) or taking a stroll down Cokkeslane or Gropecuntlane (which changed its name to Grape Street, and later on, Grub Street).

In Paris, a traveller might have found himself in Rue Trousse-Puteyne (Whore's Slit Street), Rue Grattecon (Scratch Cunt Street) or even Rue du Poileau Con (Hairy Cunt Street, now known as the more acceptable Rue de Pelecan).

The Psychology of Swearing

You'll be pleased to hear that, according to one of the world's top experts on swearing, our aptitude for swearing and cursing does not diminish with age. Timothy Jay Ph.D., Professor of Psychology at North Adams State University in Massachusetts, states that even when a debilitating illness such as Alzheimer's robs someone of their ability to communicate, the capacity to swear is almost always the last thing to go.

That's just one of the conclusions that the good professor has reached in his swearing studies and – for want of a better expression – he's pretty fucking pissed off that not enough psychologists are interested in swearing. He thinks they're too embarrassed to tackle the subject. The pussies. Another finding that Professor Jay has unearthed is that, on average, 3% of all conversations at work involve obscenities as do 13% of our conversations while we're 'at leisure'.

'Swearing is basically a way to relieve anger and frustration in a non-physical way,' says Professor Jay, and believes that it provides a useful way for us to express our dislike of someone without resorting to kicking seven shades of shit out of them.

Swear in Zulu

Visitors to Pongola (yes, this is a real place), Babanango, Nongoma – or any other town in Zululand – should make sure they take this list of phrases with them. After all, how else will you be able to tell someone that 'their pussy smells like fish' in their native tongue?

In English	In (phonetic) Zulu
Your mother's cunt	Msuno kanyoku
Cunt lips	Malebe
Faggot	Stabane
Your pussy smells like fish	Ingquza yakho inuka njengo fishi
Go eat shit	Tsa mor kaka

Smelly pussy	Ngquza enukayo
Pussy	Golo
Wet pussy	Golo eilmanzi
Your grandmother is a bitch	Ugogo wakho isfebe
Fuck	Bhebha
You love big dick	Uthanda ipipi elikhulu
Asshole	Mdidi
Whore	Sifebe
Pussy juices	Manzi egolo
Left-over shit	Sihlama

The Origins of 'Fuck'

Despite what you might have read, the word 'fuck' does not derive from the acronym 'For Unlawful Carnal Knowledge' (supposedly the words on a badge worn by convicted adulterers or prostitutes in Ye Olden Days). Nor does it derive from the phrase 'Fornication Under Consent of the King' (reflecting the need to repopulate this country after the Great Plague).

The verb to fuck is the English form of a word with origins in several Germanic languages. These include the Middle Dutch 'fokken' (to thrust), dialectical Swedish 'focka' (to strike, to push or to copulate), dialectic Norwegian 'fukka' (to copulate with) and the German 'fucken' (also to copulate).

Despite the importance of 'fuck' in the history of swearing, scholars cannot find a written example of the word before the fifteenth century (the word's first appearance in English was in 1475). One reason might be the fact that the word was so taboo that it was never written down in the Middle Ages.

The word first appeared in a dictionary in 1671 although Samuel Johnson omitted it from his own great dictionary in 1755. Fucking prude.

Harry Potter and the Filthy Vocabulary

When Spanish director Alfonso Cuaron was selected to helm the third *Harry Potter* film, he was forced to sign a special contract saying that he would not swear in front of any of the child actors.

On set, Cuaron did his best to keep his temper and when really driven to despair he swore only in Spanish.

By the end of shooting, the young cast was rumoured to be more fluent in Spanish obscenities than they were in English ones and had even taken to secretly nicknaming him *Pincho Poncho* which translates to 'that prick Alfsonso'.

Worried About Your Swearing?

Do you swear too much? Are you concerned about your 'potty mouth'? If so, then The Cuss Control Academy may be the answer to your prayers.

Founded in America (where else?), you can visit the Cuss Control Academy for practical hints and tips (including '10 Tips for Taming your Tongue' and 'So What's Wrong with Swearing?') on the web at www.cusscontrol.com.

There's even a book available called *Cuss Control: The Complete Book on How to Curb Your Cursing* by James O'Connor.

One of his helpful tips to prevent swearing at work is to 'imagine that your sweet little grandmother is always standing next to you'.

Cunts at the Dinner Table

The less educated described it as 'cunt-shaped plates' whereas the art cognoscenti recognised artist, author and feminist Judy Chicago's exhibit as a symbol of women's achievements in Western civilisation.

The plates are part of Judy's exhibit 'The Dinner Party' which, since its completion in 1979, has been seen by over a million people in six countries on three continents before taking up residence at the Brooklyn Museum of Art.

The ceramic dinnerware depicts the vulva, uterus and fallopian tubes.

And they call this art...

What a Twat!

In 1841, the great poet Robert Browning quite innocently used the word 'twat' in his famous poem 'Pippa Passes', the poem which gave us the line 'God's in his heaven – All's right with the world'.

The offending lines are as follows (to save you having to look them up in that volume of Browning you no doubt have on your shelf):

Then, owls and bats, Cowls and twats, Monks and nuns, in a cloister's moods, Adjourn to the oak-stump pantry

Apparently Browning thought it was an item of clothing worn by nuns. No-one queried it for 40 years, until the editors of the *Oxford English Dictionary* wrote to

Browning and asked him 'in what sense was he using the word'?

Browning replied he had discovered it in a 1659 poem called 'Vanity of Vanities' which went:

They talk't of his having a Cardinall's Hat;
They'd send him as soon an Old Nun's Twat.

He's therefore taken twat to mean something nuns wore on their heads...

One imagines that there was much sniggering at the *Oxford English Dictionary* before they finally set the great man straight...

The Top 10 Swear Words in Punjabi

1. Maa chodh
Motherfucker

2. Pan chodh
Sister fucker

3. Loolla
Prick

4. Choos mera loolla!
Suck my dick!

5. Bhund*
Arse

6. Bhund phuti
Ripped arse

7. Fhuddhi
Pube
(apparently also a term of endearment)

8. Tille lund di ulladh
Son of a limp dick!

9. Sala
Bastard!

10. Sala kutha
Bastard bitch!

*Bhund is also a make of Indian sauces sold in British supermarkets. It caused uproar with Punjabi speakers when it first appeared on the shelves!

Politically Correct Wanking

Experts in America, home of political correctness, all concur that the term 'jacking off' is blatantly sexist if applied to female masturbation.

The recognised politically-correct term for female masturbation is 'jilling off'.

Novelty Swearing

Looking for something to take your aggression out on after a hard day at the office? Then look no further than The Ultimate Uppercut, Swearing Punch Ball! This little punchbag actually swears back at you when you hit it, and provokes you to hit it even harder!

The Swearing Punch Ball has a vocabulary of four different phrases – 'Eat Shit', 'Fuck You', 'You're an Arsehole' and 'Fucking Jerk!'

Pussy to Lady in One Move

Under pressure from state censors and retailers, in 1985, the title of Marvin Gaye's song 'Sanctified Pussy' had to be changed to 'Sanctified Lady' for his posthumous album release, *Dream of a Lifetime*.

'Shall I Cock Piss Fuck Shit Carry This To Your Cunt Cunt Cunt Motherfucker Car, Ma'am?'

OK, we're not sure if these were the exact words spoken by grocery bagger Karl Petzold, a Tourette's Syndrome sufferer when he was fired from his job at Farmer Jack's Grocery Store in Michigan – but they are probably close.

Tourette's is a potentially life-wrecking neurological disorder which can manifest itself as an uncontrollable urge to **spit** and/or **scream swear words**. For Petzold, who had been a Tourette's sufferer since he was seven, the illness resulted in involuntary outbursts not only of obscene language, but in shouting ethnic and **religious insults**, usually in the company of those who are likely to be the most offended by the terms.

Petzold was hired by the supermarket in July 1995 and his duties put him in continual contact with the public when he was packing groceries for customers at the till and taking them to their cars.

In May 1996, Petzold was packing groceries for several black customers when he began yelling '**Fuck you**, fuck you, nigger, nigger.' Fortunately, **a fight** did not ensue, however Petzold's behaviour was reported to the store's manager, who sent the employee home and then fired him a few days later.

Petzold took the supermarket to court, claiming that his Tourette's did not affect his **ability to perform** his job and that he was protected from firing under the state's anti-discrimination laws. In a shock verdict, the court declared that Petzold's '**offensive language**, which he admitted to using on a daily basis in the presence of customers, children and other employees, made him unfit for his job as a bagger as a matter of law.'

The court went on to say that, even though Petzold's condition was **beyond his control**, it was unfair to expect his employer to overlook that condition. The judges wrote: 'We find that it would be ridiculous to expect a business to tolerate this type of language in the presence of its customers, even though we understand that it is involuntary'.

(It's not recorded what Petzold said on hearing the verdict.)

N.B. Tourette's Syndrome sufferers can still lead relatively normal lives – provided they pick an appropriate career such as professional soccer player, radio shock-jock, lead singer with a punk rock band or builder. They are NOT advised to take jobs such as Sunday school teacher, diplomat, baby photographer, bereavement counsellor or the person who announces arrivals and departures at King's Cross Station.

I Wish I'd Fucking Said That!

'The foolish and wicked practice of profane cursing and swearing is a vice so mean and low that every person of sense and character detests and despises it.'

George Washington

'Cursing is invoking the assistance of a spirit to help you inflict suffering. Swearing on the other hand, is invoking only the witness of a spirit to a statement you wish to make.'

John Ruskin

'When a gentlemen is disposed to swear, it is not for any standers-by to curtail his oaths.'

William Shakespeare

'A footman may swear; but he cannot swear like a lord. He can swear as often: but can he swear with equal delicacy, propriety, and judgment?'

Jonathan Swift

'The idea that no gentleman ever swears is all wrong. He can swear and still be a gentleman if he does it in a nice and benevolent and affectionate way.'

Mark Twain

'Take away the right to say 'fuck' and you take away the right to say 'fuck the government!'

Lenny Bruce

'Twas but my tongue, 'twas not my soul that swore.'

Euripides

Stupid Motherfuckers

It's a fact that, in 1649, Parliament passed a law against swearing at your parents. Anyone found guilty of swearing at their parents would be sentenced... to death.

(There are no readily-available records which show whether parents actually ever did turn errant children over to the law for hanging if they spoke out of turn.)

The Height of Wank

When Germans refer to 'the colossal mountain of wank', they are not usually talking about Adolf Hitler's vast magnum opus *Mein Kampf* (although they could be).

Instead, they are referring to Wank Mountain in the Bavarian Alps. 1780 metres high, you can get to the top by a cable car, which is amusingly called the Wankbahn. If you are so inclined, you can even spend the night at the summit in the hotel there. It's called the Wankhaus...

Those who don't fancy visiting Wank in person can keep an eye on it through the Wank Webcam, which provides all the latest news, views and Wank weather conditions. You can find the webcam at:

http://www.swisswebcams.ch/deutsch/webcams_detailansicht.php?wid=1045500451

Rude Cockney Rhyming Slang

Short form	Long form	Disguised word
Almond	Almond Rock	Cock
Berkeley	Berkeley Hunt	Cunt
Bottle	Bottle and Glass	Arse
Brighton	Brighton Rock	Cock
Bristols	Bristol Cities	Titties
Cattle	Cattle Truck	Fuck
Cobblers	Cobbler's Awls	Balls
Cuddled	Cuddled and Kissed	Pissed

Elephant	Elephant and Castle	**Arsehole**
Feather	Feather Plucker	**Fucker**
Friar	Friar Tuck	**Fuck**
Goose	Goose and Duck	**Fuck**
Grumble	Grumble and Grunt	**Cunt**
Hampton	Hampton Wick	**Prick**
Hit	Hit and Miss	**Piss**
Horse	Horse and Trap	**Crap**
J. Arthur	J. Arthur Rank	**Wank**
Joe	Joe Hunt	**Cunt**
Khyber	Khyber Pass	**Arse**
Orchestras	Orchestra Stalls	**Balls**
Pheasant	Pheasant Plucker	**Fucker**
Pony	Pony and Trap	**Crap**
Russian	Russian Duck	**Fuck**
Tom	Tom Tit	**Shit**
	Uncle Dick	**Prick**

Inside Miss World

Back in the days when the Miss World contest was still broadcast live and commanded a global audience of many, many millions, a contestant from a nation that shall remain nameless stepped forward to do her two minute live interview. English was most certainly not her first language and, for some reason (perhaps a bitchy rival contestant had told her), she was convinced that the singular of 'countries' was 'cunt'.

All credit goes to the interviewer who kept his composure as the hapless beauty contestant came out with lines like 'My cunt is very beautiful place', 'I invite everyone to come and visit my cunt one day' and 'I want to work with underprivileged children in my cunt'...

Not surprisingly, this clip has never turned up on Denis Norden's *It'll Be Alright on the Night*...

Swearing Is Bad For You – It's Official

Russian scientist Gennady Cheurin, Head of Yekaterinburg's Centre for Ecological Safety and Survival, believes that regular swearing can have terrible effects on us all. According to his findings, men who swear become impotent while women who use more than the occasional cuss word get transformed into men.

Cheurin's team made this astounding discovery after swearing at a glass of water for several hours non-stop and then pouring it over wheat seeds. Only 48% of those seeds watered with 'sworn-at' water germinated, compared with 93% watered with 'clean' water. (It's amazing what you can get a grant for these days.) A follow-up study of self-confessed 'heavy swearers' showed many of the men suffered erectile dysfunction, while the women were hairier and more muscular than usual.

Sounds like a load of fucking bollocks to me (oops – there goes my sex life for a week...)

Spot the Swear Word

Cunningly concealed in each of the following well-known texts is a hidden, but well-known swearword. Can YOU identify it?

'Daffodils' by William Wordsworth:

I wander'd lonely as a cloud
That floats on high o'er vales and hills,
When all at once I saw a cunt
A host, of golden daffodils.

Hamlet by William Shakespeare:

'Alas, poor Yorick! I knew him, Horatio: a fellow of infinite jest, of most excellent fancy. He hath borne me on his motherfucking back a thousand times.'

The Theory of Relativity by Albert Einstein:

$e = mc^{fuck}$

Jerusalem by William Blake:

And did those feet in ancient time
Walk upon England's bollocks green?
And was the Holy Lamb of God
On England's pleasant pastures seen?

The Declaration of Independence:

We hold these truths to be self-evident, that all men are created equal, that they are endowed by their Creator with certain unalienable Rights, that among these are Life, Liberty and the pursuit of shit.

'I Have A Dream' speech by Martin Luther King Jr.:

I have a dream that my four little children will one day live in a nation where they will not be judged by the color of their piss but by the content of their character.

Coming to a Cinema Near You...

There are those that say Bollywood will soon break into the British mainstream and be enjoyed en-masse by a non-Asian audience. Well, not on the evidence of a film released in the UK in 2003 it won't. Non-Asians passing by their local Asian cinemas were startled to see huge banners and posters for a new Bollywood blockbuster.

Called *Jism.*

It seems that no-one had bothered to tell anyone involved with the film's distribution that *Jism* meant something quite different in English. (To Asian audiences, it kind of translates to 'guts'.)

Despite its seeming promise of hard core pornographic scenes and 'money shots' a-plenty, even *Jism*, directed by Amit Saxena and starring John Abraham, Bipasha Basu and Gulshan Grover failed to draw in that elusive crossover audience.

Better luck with *Cum-gargling Madrapoor Minxes*, boys...

The Wit and Wisdom of Jim Morrison

Rock poet Jim Morrison once composed the following charming ode which he delivered to an assembled group of his female fans:

'You're all a bunch of fucking idiots. Your faces are being pressed into the shit of the world. Take your fucking friend and love him. Do you want to see my cock?'

Inscrutable Slang

Have you ever wondered what the Japanese call what we in the West rather insensitively nickname the Jap's Eye?

Apparently, they call it The German Mouth because it is never seen to smile.

The Cunt Coloring Book

This American book, illustrated by Tee Corrine, contains beautiful (and extremely graphic) illustrations of the vagina, all ready to be coloured in.

As the blurb for the book says: 'Gorgeous black line drawings invite you to grab your Crayolas and color away!'

(And you thought the only cunt in a book was a jacket photo of Will Self.)

18 Downright Nasty Names for your Penis

A recent survey carried out among men in the US reported the most popular names for their penis. These included friendly or pet names like 'Little Man', 'Pecker', 'Lollipop', 'Tool', 'John Thomas', 'Sausage' and of course 'Willy', however the following were considered the most offensive:

1. Prick
2. Cock
3. Fuck Stick
4. Cunt Stabber
5. Cunt Plug
6. Throbbing Sugar Stick
7. One-eyed Trouser Trout
8. Raw Salami
9. Love Spurter
10. Love Pump / Pumper

11.Baby's Arm

12.Bald-headed Candidate

13.Pink Torpedo

14.Man Meat

15.Big Blue Veiner

16.Oral Tube

17.Warhead

18.Cum Gun

Keeping Score in Raw

Eddie Murphy is one of the most enthusiastic and spirited swearers you'd ever see in the movies, (although, it must be said, his Dr Doolittle films have been very disappointing in this respect). The following is a list of the expletives that can be heard in Raw, the 1987 film of one of his New York stand-up concerts.

Expletive	No. of times uttered
Shit	103
Fuck	92
Motherfucker/s	56
Ass	50

Fucking	39
Dick	33
Fucked Up / Fucked	28
Pussy	28
Motherfucking	22
Bitch	18
Goddamn / Damn	17
Nigger	11
Bullshit	4
Faggots	3

TOTAL

504 expletives in **93** minutes

Foul Language

If you think Arsenal and Spurs are bitter rivals then you should go to Serbia and watch the clubs Zvezda and the Partizans play each other. When Zvezda fans score a goal or win a match they display huge banners that say: 'Nase sreçi nigde kraja, grobari nam lizu jaja!' – which translates as 'There's no end to our luck, the gravediggers are licking our balls!'

(No. We're not sure what it meant either but there aren't many places you can write about gravediggers licking your balls.)

Fucking Austrians

When you think of fucking Austrians you probably think of Arnold Schwarzenegger and Adolf Hitler, but you could equally be thinking of the inhabitants of a small Austrian village called Fucking.

Oh yes, it really exists. It isn't an urban myth. The country that gave us delicious chocolate cakes and Nazi ideology has also given us the place with one of the world's rudest names.

Located at 48' 03" N 13' 51"E (for those with a good atlas and too much time on their hands), the normally-peaceful village has been plagued in recent years

by British tourists stealing the road signs*
– especially the one imploring drivers
to slow down and which translates to
'Fucking. Not so fast, please!' (*Fucking:
Bitte — nicht so schnell!*).

The village recently held a vote to change
its name – but the motion was defeated.
The Mayor of Fucking Siegfried Hoeppl
said, 'Everyone here knows what it means
in English, but for us Fucking is Fucking
– and it's going to stay Fucking.'

By the way – no-one seems to know what
the correct term for an inhabitant of
Fucking is. 'Fuckers' sounds right.

*Mayor Siegfried Hoeppel, says that he
hopes to make the signs more secure from
theft through 'bigger, longer screws'....

Unusual Swearing from Around the World

(Phonetically, to make it nice and easy for you)

Din mamma suger björnar i skogen!

Your mother sucks bears in the forest

(Swedish)

Elif air ab tizak!

1,000 cocks up your arse!

(Arabic)

Tiu nia ma chow hai

Fuck your mother's smelly cunt

(Cantonese)

Vas faire foutre à la vache

Go fuck a cow

(French)

Ou lun dun jhew hai

Ox cock boiled in pig spunk

One presumes this is an insult and not a recipe...

(Cantonese)

Jou ma se wildebees siflis biltong poes

Your mother's cunt is like a dried-up syphilitic Wildebeest's

(Afrikaans)

Eyreh be afass seder emmak

My cock in your mother's ribcage

(Arabic)

Cago en tu leche

I shit in your milk

(Spanish)

Gamo tin havra sou je ton kapike sou

I fuck your family and its place of origin

(Cypriot)

Sut mine rådne løg

Suck my hairy onions!

(Danish)

Äitisi nai poroja

Your mother fucks with reindeers

(Finnish)

Pod marani!

Professional arse-fucker!

(Bengali)

Tere bahin ki shalwaar main thook phainkun

I spit in your sister's trousers

(Urdu)

Chippkali ke jhaant ke paseene

Sweat of a lizard's pubes!

(Hindi)

Te másodosztályú geci!

You are sperm from the lower classes

(Hungarian)

Zozo ou gro tankou yon tik tak

You're hung like a *Tic-Tac*

(Haitian)

Din mor var god i nat, men din far var bedre!

Your mum was great last night – but your dad was better

(Danish)

Longekranke Wikser

Lung-sick wanker!

(Luxembourgish)

Issunboshi!

One inch boy!

(Japanese)

Teri maa ki kuss may gadha paadey

A donkey farts in your mother's arse

(Urdu)

Aperonk!

Monkey masturbator!

(Norwegian)

Bur ki chatani!

Cunt ketchup!

(Hindi)

Sandas maa baiseli ghilodi ni gaand na vaad par na pasina ne chaat

Lick the sweat off the lizard's ass hair which is in the toilet

(Gujerati)

Ananin amina beton dokerim, butun mahle abaza kalir trans

I will pour concrete into your mum's pussy and the entire neighbourhood will become horny

(Turkish)

The Origin of the V Sign

The origin of the American 'one fingered gesture' is pretty clear as is the 'wanking gesture' popularised in the 1970s by coffee spokesman Gareth Hunt – but the good old British V sign is a lot more baffling. What sexual act can it possibly refer to?

The answer is that it doesn't. Its origins aren't sexual at all. The V sign was first used by English bowmen around the time of the Battle of Agincourt. When the French took bowmen prisoner, they would sever the two fingers the archer used to draw back their bow strings – and then released them. English archers who still had their fingers would let their French enemies know by frantically making the V sign at the opposing army before battle commenced.

During World War Two, Winston Churchill used a reversed, palm-forward version of the gesture as a 'victory' sign. However, being fond of the odd dram or two, he would quite often muddle the two gestures up and end up flicking the Vs at his own troops...

Incidentally, one obscene hand gesture now growing in popularity is to raise your hand in the air with the palm towards you, with *all* your fingers sticking upwards. To avoid any misunderstanding due to the person you are insulting not knowing the gesture, you should also mutter a casual 'treat the family!'

They're Rude – it's Official

Before 1972, the *Oxford English Dictionary* refused to carry the words fuck or cunt – which left generations of naughty schoolboys severely disappointed and forced to look up much duller words like bum and willy instead...

All Out Brothers!

It didn't take much to provoke the British Leyland workforce to strike in the early '80s. So it was probably not surprising that car production came to a grinding halt in 1982 when one of the company's chief executives described his workers as 'fucking bastards and fucking working class pigs'.

This is the only known incidence of swearing-related industrial action in the UK. However, several years later in Saudi Arabia, a British worker was subjected to 40 lashes in a public square after telling his boss to 'Stuff it up your fat arse, you old wanker'.

American Wankers

It's true. America is full of wankers – and they're totally unembarrassed by it. Wank is not a recognised word in American English – which is good news for all those in Britain who like a cheap laugh at the expense of total strangers.

For example, in New York there is a practicing dentist named Daniel Wank (you can supply your own dentist/masturbatory joke here) and in 1994, the official Republican Spokesman for the state of Minnesota went by the name of Randy Wanke.

3 Offensive Australian Terms for an 'Easy Lay'

(well, more offensive than 'easy lay', that is)

Walk-up Fuck

(i.e. all a man needs to do is walk up to her and ask)

Turtle

(as in 'Once she's on her back, she's fucked')

Box of Assorted Creams

(Box = vagina, Cream = semen)

Anal Astronauts and 34 Other Slang Words for Arse Pirates

1. Anal Astronaut

2. Arse Pirate

3. Back-Door Commando

4. Battie-Boy

5. B.B.
(abbreviation for Bum Boy)

6. Booty Bandit

7. Brown Dirt Cowboy

8. Bufu
(shortened form of Buttfucker)

9. Cackpipe Commando

10. Chocolate Runway Pilot

11. Chutney Farmer

12. Cocoa Shunter

13. Colon Choker

14. Donut-Puncher

15. Fudge-Nudger

16. Haemorrhoid Hitman

17. Hitchhiker on the
Hershey Highway

18. Jobby Jouster

19. Marmite Driller

20. Mister Rimmington

21. Mud-Packer

22. Navigator of the
Windward passage

23. Pile-Driver

24. Poo Pusher

25. Rectal Ranger

26. Ring Raider

27. Ringpiece Romeo

28. Sausage Smuggler

29. Shirt Lifter

30. Shit Miner

31. Shit-Stabber

32. Sperm Burper

33. Turd Bandit

34. Turd-Burglar

35. Turdinator

How to Tell Someone to 'Fuck off!' in Hawaiian

If you're being harassed in Honolulu or molested in Maui then just say:

'E ho'opohole 'oe i ko'u mai'a'

This means 'Fuck off!' although the literal translation is actually 'Peel back the skin of my banana.'

Acronyms Using the Word Fuck

AMF

Adios, Motherfucker

ASAFP

As Soon As Fucking Possible

BFD

Big Fucking Deal

BUF

Big Ugly Fucker
(US Air Force slang for the Boeing B-52
Stratofortress)

DILLIGAFF

Does It Look Like I Give A Flying Fuck?

FNG

Fucking New Guy
(US military term; a new recruit to a
combat unit)

FTW

Fuck The World
(Hell's Angels' slogan)

FUBB

Fucked Up Beyond Belief
(Originally military slang)

Also **FUBAR**:
Fucked Up Beyond All Recognition

FUBISO

Fuck You Buddy, I'm Shipping Out
(US Army slang)

GFU

General Fuck Up
(US military slang)

MF

Motherfucker

RTFM

Read The Fucking Manual
(also the name of a Q&A column in *MacUser*
magazine)

SNAFU

Situation Normal, All Fucked Up
(US army slang for a botched or confused
situation)

TARFU

Things Are Really Fucked Up
(as above)

'Take out your intestines and fuck them'

and other inventive Armenian swearing…

'Motherfucker', 'Fucking cunt', 'Fuck off and die!' – it's all very uncreative compared to some of the phrases they use in Armenia…

I fuck your soul

Kunem ko hokey

I'll cum in your eyes 'til you go blind

Jhajh dam achkit minchev gooyranas

I shove an oily fish up your ass

Yooghot dzuk khrem vored

I'll rip your nuts off and fling them to your face with a slingshot

Dzeveret ke ketrem, ragatkov gelxeet ke kerakem

You smell like shit

Kaki bes ge hodiss

Let the rats cum on you

Krisnera zhazh tan vred

Take out your intestines and fuck them

Aghiknered hani kuni

Your ass is full of cum

Vored zhazhov leekena

Fucked Whore

Kunvatz Agarka

Suck my shit

Kaks tstses

Shit on your grandmother

Kakem teerojit mera

Eat my pussy hair

Ptzi Mazes Beranit Mech

Eat my dick on an empty stomach

Anoti porov geleris ger

Your mum's so fat because she ate a lot of cum

Ar es erku dolare toor mameet asa erek gisher lav er

Here - eat your pizza with my cum

Ar pizzas zhazhees het ker

Why is your mum dead? Did she suck a horse's cock and choke on the cum?

Hera mamad mere? dzee-ee kleer tztzav zhazhitz khekhtvav?

Pour my diarrhoea on your face

Lootzatz kakes Itznem ereseek

The Great Anti-Swearing Petition

In January 2005, Chris Topher proposed a petition on the website www.petitionspot.com to ban swearing. His plea read:

'Swearing is evil, and should be stopped, that is why I propose that it should be banned from all public places!!!

Children are learning to swear very young these days, and that is a very worrying fact!!!

Here is my Proposed list of Banned Swear Words:

Fuck
Shit
Cunt
Nigger'

Among the responses he received were:

'Cunt Cunt fucking nigga. FUCK OFF! That is the most fucking stupid petition I have ever heard. Shit isn't even a bad word. Here's a situation, is it better to say ohh darn I just slammed my finger with a hammer accidentally, or say ohhhhhh shit I hit my hand. Sometimes you need a swear word. Fuck you motherfucker haha.'

'I NEVER FUCKING CUSSED IN MY LIFE!!!!!!!!!!!! (from someone logging on as fuckshitcocksuckerdamnbitch)'

'**Fuck you fucking wankers** you can't stand fucking swearing cus you're fucking motherfuckers who wank other motherfuckers for the sake for fucking.'

'**ALL THOSE CUNTS THAT SWEAR SHOULD BE FUCKING SHOT!!** FUCKING MOTHER FUCKING MOTHER FUCKING COCKSUCKERS!!! ALL OF YOU!!! SHOT DEAD FUCKING DEAD BITCH!!! FUCKING FOUL FUCKING MOUTHED COCK CUSTARD EATING PUSSY FUCKERS!!!'

'**I agree.** Only rude people would use vulgar words.'

'**Fuck no bitch shit!! damn!!** I do agree that the n word is bad though!! Shit!!!'

'Get a life if u seriously fink ne1 is g2 sign dis 4 any reason other dan swearin @ u. & just 4 ur enjoyment·· fuck u prick-ass dumb shit motherfucking cock-face wanker fag-skeaze!'

A Selective Count of Count of Swear Words in Three Great Literary Works

	Lady Chatterley's Lover by D H Lawrence	Ulysses by James Joyce	Finnegan's Wake by James Joyce
Fuck	30	2	0
Cunt	14	1	0
Balls	13	3	10
Shit	6	4	1
Arse	3	10	1
Piss	3	4	1

N.B. This takes into account exact words, and does not include variants such as 'shite', or 'cunty', both of which appear four times in *Ulysses*.

Making an Arse of Yourself

According to the UK-based *Asian News* in May 2004, a man arrested in Cheetham on drugs charges was called Mr Anus Butt. Wonder where he hid his stash...

(For those of you who think we make this up, check out:
http://www.theasiannews.co.uk/news/index/11232.html)

'Yippee Ki-yay Mister Falcon!

*and other examples of
stupid movie censorship*

Depending on where and when a film is being shown on TV, the local network will censor it to varying degrees. In most cases, swear words will be muted or bleeped – but in some instances, the broadcaster will re-dub the film, which just draws attention to the censored words even more. These are some of the worst, mainly from US or Canadian broadcasts:

'Flip you, you flipping airhead'

Fuck you, you fucking dickhead
Lethal Weapon

'Yippee ki-yay mister falcon!'

Yippee ki-yay motherfuckers!
Die Hard 2

'You racist melon farmer!'

You racist motherfucker!
Die Hard 3

'Hand me the keys you Fairy Godmother!'

Hand me the keys you fucking cocksucker!

The Usual Suspects

'Forget you, you motherforgetter!'

Fuck you, you motherfucker!

Casino

'Come on maggot farmer!'

Come on, motherfucker!

Platoon

'Mothercrusher'

Motherfucker
Robocop

'Forget you dad!'

Fuck you dad!
The Breakfast Club

'I'd freak Elvis'

I'd fuck Elvis
True Romance

'Nice one'

Nice beaver
Naked Gun

'Mutual funding money'

Motherfucking money

Jackie Brown

'This is what happens when you take a Frenchman up the Alps!'

This is what happens when you fuck a stranger in the ass!

The Big Lebowski

'Why the heck did you do that, dipstick?'

Why the hell did you do that, dipshit?

Dumb and Dumber

'Mother hubbard!'

Motherfucker!
Pulp Fiction

'Clean my clock!'

Suck my cock!
Thelma and Louise

'I'd marry me.
I'd marry me hard!'

I'd fuck me, I'd fuck me hard!
Silence of the Lambs

You're Fukt!

If you're travelling in Sweden you might be mystified to see one of those large roadside electronic signs that gives the temperature, also displaying something like: 'Fukt 82%'. This isn't telling you the rate of virginity in the area you're visiting – the word 'fukt' bizarrely just means 'humidity'. (You can buy Fukt Creme in some pharmacies in Sweden, although this is a hand cream and not, as its name implies, their version of KY Gel.)

Cuntfest!

Not a description of an Al-Qaeda Conference, but an event held at Penn State University in November 2001.

The feminist organisers of 'CUNTFEST!' found themselves (not surprisingly) at the centre of controversy when they held this event, billed as an empowering day of celebration and a reclamation of the 'C' word, which, according to author Inga Muscio in her book *Cunt: A Declaration of Independence*, was actually a 'title of respect for women, priestesses and witches'.

The event had been approved by the University Park Allocation Committee but from the beginning there was trouble. UPAC wanted to change the event name and the *Daily Collegian* refused to print ads which said CUNTFEST! in big bold letters. Penn State Police removed a large banner that said CUNTFEST! but the event organisers insisted that the banner be re-hung because they had written permission to hang it from the ironically-named 'Osmond Building' on campus. The banner was re-hung, then stolen, and a second one also went missing.

Berks

The next time you call someone a Berk – watch out! The term is actually a lot ruder than you may realise.

(Berk is actually Cockney rhyming slang from the phrase 'Berkshire Hunt'. So, it's actually Cockney for cunt. Nice that the word cunt and the hunting fraternity are still so closely associated after all these years...)

Shock Horror! – Truth Told in Parliament!

In March 2004, Prime Minister Tony Blair sat down at his House of Commons table – only to find someone had carved '*Tony Blair is a cunt*' into its historic surface. Extensive investigations to find the culprit proved fruitless (probably because there were just too many likely suspects...).

In an uncannily similar act of political subversion, shortly before the Iraq War Ali G (aka comedian Sacha Baron-Cohen) managed to get hold of Kofi Annan's personal notepad in the UN General Assembly and scrawl on it the immortal line *'Saddam Hussein is a bell end – sort him out.'*

Some Bollocks from Blue

Boy band Blue apparently had a pre-show warm-up routine where they all held hands in a little circle and then screamed '1, 2, 3, bollocks!' four times in succession. The origins of this ritual are not known. Speculation as to whether it referred to the quality of their imminent performance is entirely up to you.

(Completely irrelevant aside: In Russian, the word 'blue' is slang for 'gay'...)

Cunt – The Origin

The roots of our *other* favourite four letter word most probably go back to the Latin *Cunnus,* which meant vagina. From there it evolved into the German *Kunton* and the Norse *Kunta.*

The use of the word in the English language has been successfully tracked back to around 1325, However, earlier than this, Parish records show women named Gunoka Cuntles (1219) and Bele Wydcunthe (1328). Men too had some unfortunate names including a Godwin Clawecuncte (1066), Simon Sitbithecunte (1167) and John Fillecunt (1246).

Chaucer used the word 'cunt' in 'The Miller's Tale' but spelled in the old English form of 'queynte' (one of the characters is chatting up Hemde Nicolas's wife and then '**grabbed her by the queynte**'). At the time also meant 'a pleasing or lovely thing' – which is why it evolved into the modern word 'quaint'.

The use of the word **cunt** as an insulting way to refer to a woman is actually believed to be a much later thing. In fact it's more likely to be from the twentieth-century, with experts tracing the first known use of cunt in that sense only as far back as 1929 in America.

The reason that cunt is now considered the strongest swear word of them all is because of the **sexist connotations** it contains. People today are far more offended by words that carry sexist and/or racist implications than by ones which simply refer to **sex acts or organs**.

In a recent survey among 1,033 members of the general public aged 18 and over across all social classes, 2% of respondents aged 18-34 thought that the word 'cunt' was not swearing, and 5% thought it was '**mild**'.

Brad Cock

In the English-speaking world, the name Brad Pitt may be very advantageous to any movie that's opening – but in Sweden it's an entirely different story and his name on a movie poster is guaranteed to provoke howls of laughter.

'Pitt' in Swedish is a very rude slang word for 'cock'.

Regrets – I've had a few...

In England we say 'If only I could turn back time' after doing something we regret. The Serbians, however, have a far more colourful expression for this: 'Da bi sel v pizdo materno!', meaning 'If only I could crawl back into my mother's cunt.'

Cack-pants Aldrin

Buzz Aldrin, crew member of Apollo 11 – which made the first manned landing of the Moon back in 1969 – was by all accounts rather pissed off that he didn't get to be the first man to walk on the Moon's surface. At the last minute, his commander, Neil Armstrong, pulled rank and decided that *he* was going to grab the glory.

Still, Buzz did manage to get himself into the record books when he became the first man to *swear* on the Moon with the immortal line, 'Bloody hell – I've just taken a shit in my space suit.'

Overpriced Shit

Presumably, exquisite and expensive perfume by Coco Chanel does not sell very well in Brazil. In that country Coco (spelled *coqueau* but pronounced coco) means shit. This may also explain how Coco the Clown got his name...

Dirty Sanchez

So you thought it was just a juvenile TV programme. Wrong. Dirty Sanchez is actually slang for the act of sticking a finger (or your cock) up another person's arsehole (usually while they are asleep or otherwise out of it) and then smearing shit all over their top lip to give them the appearance of having a moustache.

This is by all accounts neither a popular nor sexually rewarding act and is probably limited to groups of blokes sharing a room on Club 18–30 holidays.

Bollocks – The Origin

Where does the term 'bollocks' come from, in the sense of 'rubbish' or 'nonsense' – as in 'that's complete 'bollocks'?

When the Sex Pistols' album, *Never Mind the Bollocks, Here's The Sex Pistols* went on sale in 1977, the manager of the Virgin record store in Nottingham was charged under the 1889 Indecent Advertisements Act for displaying a poster for the LP in his shop window.

At the subsequent trial, a Professor of Linguistics was called upon to define the word bollocks. He explained that it was actually an eighteenth-century nickname for priests. Because priests typically talked such drivel in their sermons, the word bollocks eventually became synonymous with rubbish.

What's in a name?

The president of award-winning IT company D·Link Inc. based in Irvine, California, is one Mr Wonder Wang. (It makes you wonder if, somewhere in China, there's a Caucasian boss whose name translates in Mandarin to Mr Fantastic Cock.)

(While we're on the subject, the CEO of Koc Holding is one Mr Mustafa Koc.)

Swearing in the Universal Language

It's reassuring to learn that even when Esperanto, the so-called 'universal language', was being developed, the inventors were far-sighted enough to pepper it with a few choice swear words.

English	Esperanto
Asshole	Anusulo
Cunt	Pico
Fuck off!	Forfikigi
Idiot	Kreteno

Motherfucker	Patrinfikulo
Shit	Merdo
Slut	Malcastulino
Son of a bitch	Putinfilaco
Whore	Publikulino

Avoiding the Swear Box – Useful Tame Euphemisms to Use

Most workplaces now have swear boxes to discourage their staff from using obscenities around the office. To help save you money, we've compiled this helpful guide to mild and acceptable alternatives to swear words.

Blow
Blast!
Damn!
Tarnation!
Dash it!
Cripes!
Crikey!
Ruddy
Cor-love-a-duck!
(Although, thinking about that one...)

Gee whiz!
Gee willickers
Poo!

Poop!
Pish!
Pish-tush!
That's piffle!

Alternatively, you could just substitute the names of appropriate celebrities for your favourite swear words.

Some useful examples:

'I hate that guy. He's a real Jim Davidson.'

'I wish I hadn't had that chicken Madras. My George Galloway feels like it's on fire.'

'I like a girl with big
Ant & Decs.'

'That idea is 100% Bernard
Manning – and you know it.'

Filthy Lucre

Before the Euro was given its present name, it was all set to be called the Ecu. That is, until the Portuguese pointed out that – in their language – *ecu* means arse.

Even the Typeface is Filthy...

It's not what you say, it's the way that you say it – especially if you use a typeface called:

FROSTBITTEN WANKER

Designed by the Reverend Josh Wilhem, it's described as an 'all capitals font with a pile of snow atop each slightly rounded character and highlights along most letters'. You can download it for your PC or Mac at:

http://desktoppub.about.com/library/fonts/dd/uc_frostbittenwanker.htm

Famous Names Altered to Make Gratuitous Swear Words

PAUL WANKA

DONALD FUCK

COCK HUDSON

CHARLES DICKENDS

DIANA TOSS AND THE
SUPREMES

ADOLF SHITLER

FELLATIO NELSON

LEON SPUNKS

SOPHIE FUCKER

ARSEY BUSSELL

BRUCE RINGSTEEN

ALAN BALLS

KNOBBY STILES

JEAN-PAUL FARTRE

SEMENEM

HELMET KOHL

FART GARFUNKEL

MALCOLM BUGGERIDGE

SANDRA BOLLOCK

LARRY SHAGMAN

CLITTLE AND LARGE

DONALD CUMSFELD

WANK WILLIAMS

DIANA FRIGG

EDITH TITWELL

PRICK WAKEMAN

ALEXANDER GRAHAM
BELLEND

KEANU CUNT

The Diplomatic Approach

For years, we've been sniggering at the fact that the Germans refer to their proud nation as the *Farterland*. Not so well known, however, is the fact that the German word for embassy is *botschaft* and the German ambassador is officially called the *botschafter.*

The De-Sexing of Fuck

John Ayto, editor of the Oxford Dictionary of Slang, has stated that the word 'fuck' has lost most of its original sexual meaning. 'Fuck is a sexual term but realistically, it is almost never used that way. The overwhelming amount of times it is being used in some figurative sense – "I'm fucking tired" or "We got fucked on that deal". I think it would be too much to say that fuck doesn't offend anybody. But its impact is diminishing at a rapid rate. Young people tend not to think of it as offensive at all.'

Google – More Than a Search Engine, More of a Sex Organ

It's very doubtful that anyone associated with setting up the super successful Internet search engine Google could possibly have known that the term had a much older – and filthier meaning...

According to that authority Dr. Samuel Johnson, google in old Anglo-Saxon actually means cunt.

No lesser figure than Alfred the Great is recorded to have used it as an insult when he taunted King Guthrum of the Vikings before the Battle of Slaughterford with the immortal taunt of 'Only your grandmother's google is great!'

How to Swear at French People

There are many in our modern day society who say that swearing is a pointless and futile activity. There may be some truth in this – but not when it comes to insulting the French. Very little can give more pleasure than swearing at a French person. Here are some choice phrases you may wish to use quite casually on your next hop over the Channel for cheap booze and fags:

Va te faire enculer!

Go get fucked up the arse!

Faut péter dans l'eau pour faire des bulles!

Go and fart in water and make bubbles!

Tu es fils d'un gay et d'une pute

Your father's a fag and your mother's a prostitute

Je te pisse en zig-zags au raie de cul!

I piss in zig-zags on your arse crack!

Parle-moi à la main

Talk to the hand

Je suis fier de mon cul quand je vois ta gueule

Seeing your face makes me proud of my arse

Enculeur de porcs!

Pig-fucker!

Emmerdeur!

Shit for brains!

Branleur!

Wanker!

Léche mon cul!

Lick my arsehole!

Tu pues la merde!

You stink of shit!

Chatte!

Cunt!

Va te faire foutre, trouduc!

Fuck off, you arsehole!

Arrête de parler, merde de tête!

Shut up, shithead!

Enculé de ta race entière!

You have been buggered by your entire race!

Calisse que t'est laid! Est-ce que ta mère t'as chié?

Fuck you're ugly – did your mother shit you out?

More American Wankers

Dirty-minded British tourists to America go out of their way to visit Wanker's Corner in Clackamas County, Oregon.

Positioned at the intersection of Borland Road and Stafford Road – if you really want to find it – you can wine and dine at Wanker's Corner Saloon and Café or buy provisions at Wanker's Country Store. The country store is apparently run by one Lois Wanker, whose unfortunately-named grandfather settled in the area in 1895.

She prefers the pronunciation *wonker* (well you would, wouldn't you?).

The Saloon is far more switched on to the place's outrageous name and offers T-shirts with the slogan 'Grab your nuts at Wanker's Corner'. They call it 'Wankerwear' and you can visit their website at www.wankerscorner.com

(For those who are conversant with American slang, you might like to know that Oregon is officially designated The Beaver State.)

Gained in Translation

Good news! According to *The Times*, Britain is finally closing its enormous trade deficit with Japan. For years, they've been selling us ugly cars and brain-rot-inducing computer games. But now, the Japanese have finally discovered something of ours worth importing – our obscenities!

In a land where applying make-up in public or swinging an umbrella is considered almost as rude and socially unacceptable as getting your cock out in the street, there is a shortage of really choice swear words. Even their hottest home-grown obscenity '*Shine Bakayaro*' translates approximately as 'Drop dead you fool!'

Little wonder then that the Japanese are now looking Westwards for new tools to express their displeasure at their fellows. The most popular import at the moment is apparently 'Fakkyuu'. Can 'Kunto-san' be very far behind?

N.B. The relative scarcity of swearing or profanity in Japan might be due to the Japanese belief in 'Kotodama', which means word spirits. It is thought that if 'bad' words are spoken or written, they can summon up evil Kotodama, who will bring harm to the person swearing. Some Japanese believe this. Others say 'What a load of fucking bollocks.'

Cunts in Music

Not a reference to Girls Aloud, but a short list of songs featuring the word:

'Lady Love Your Cunt'
by the UK band SMASH

'Just Like A Cunt' and 'A Cunt Like You'
by 1980s UK 'power electronics' group Whitehouse*

'I Might Be A Cunt, But I'm Not A Fucking Cunt'

by Australian band TISM, released in 1998 (the group's name is an acronym of 'This Is Serious Mum')

'Anal Cunt'

by G G Allin (not by the group of the same name)

What is it about cunts and Australia (apart from the fact that most of them live there)? *Cunt* was the name of a 2001 album by Australian grindcore band, Blood Duster while group TISM released an album called *Australia The Lucky Cunt*.

*Incidentally, Whitehouse had a compilation album titled *The Cream Of The Second Coming* (well, it made us laugh...).

Get Knotted!

US author, sailor and artist Clifford W. Ashley used the term 'cuntline' in his classic *The Ashley Book of Knots*, ISBN 0385040253. The cuntline denotes the groove between adjacent strands of twisted rope.

A 'cunt splice' however is a form of knot used in the rigging of ships, to join two ropes. It is stronger than a 'single splice' (so now you know).

Rude Science

Check out these substances – which are all 100% real:

Anol

Anol is another term for the molecule 4-(1-propenyl)phenol which is used in the flavour industry.

Arsole

This is the arsenic equivalent of pyrrole, and believe it or not, it's what's known as a 'ring' molecule. If you have more time on your hands than you know what to do with, check out the 1983 scientific paper "Studies on the Chemistry of the Arsoles" by G. Markl and H. Hauptmann, in the Journal of Organometallic Chemistry 248: 269.

Arsenolite

Known also as cubic arsenic trioxide, this is a naturally occurring mineral, which is also the primary product whenever arsenic ores are smelted.

Bastardane

The proper name of this molecule is 'ethano-bridged noradamantane'.

Clitorin

This molecule is a flavenol glycoside.

Dickite

Dickite is a clay-like mineral used in ceramics, glossy paper, paint filler and rubber. It was named after the geologist Dr. W. Thomas Dick, of Lanarkshire, Scotland who discovered it in the 1890s.

Fukalite

This mineral gets its name from the Fuka mine in the Fuka area of southern Japan. It is very rare, and is a form of calcium silico-carbonate.

Fucitol

This is an alcohol, whose other names are L-fuc-ol or 1-deoxy-D-galactitol. Its name is derived from the sugar fucose.

Kunzite

This is a pink mineral, not named after the vagina, but after the gemologist G.F. Kunz, the gem buyer for Tiffany & Co. who discovered it in 1902. There's an 880 carat example on display at the Smithsonian Institute in Washington DC. Now that's what we call a massive kunzite.

Vaginatin

This molecule derives its name from the plant Selinum Vaginatum.

Curse Free TV

In June 1999 the Reverand Jonas Robertson, pastor of the Abundant Life Pentecostal Church in New Orleans, launched a device that can delete pre-programmed expletives from TV programmes and movies while you're watching them.

Robertson developed the device after getting fed-up of hearing foul language on his TV and introduced it to the public at the annual convention of the 32 million member Assemblies of God denomination. Called 'Curse Free TV' (CFTV), the product can detect 150 offensive words or phrases and instantly mute the audio signal or else replace the swear word with a substitute that's stored in the machine's memory.

The device works by detecting words on the closed captioned broadcast signal so it only works with this type of programme. Original old movies and live broadcasts would, therefore, not be affected by CFTV.

Since its introduction the device has been featured in various Christian television programmes and magazines and was one of the hottest new items sold at the Christian Booksellers Association.

Lost in Translation

The Japanese car company Mitsubishi spent a fortune preparing to launch a new model called the Pajero on to the market in Spain.

Only at the very last minute did they discover that Pajero meant Wanker in Spanish. They renamed the car the Montero.

(You'd have thought they'd have learned their lesson from the General Motors model named the Nova. In Spanish *no va* means 'doesn't go'.)

The Landlord is A. Wanker

Episode 8 of the Robin Williams sitcom *Mork and Mindy* is particularly highly regarded by aficionados of television swearing – because it introduced a brand new character to the show – an evil landlord named Arnold Wanker.

Now, when you introduce a new character into a TV show, it's the 'done thing' to mention his name as many times as humanly possible – just so the audience can learn his name. Hence, the script for this particular episode was absolutely chock full of lines like 'Nanoo Nanoo, Mr. Wanker', 'Mindy, this is our landlord, Mr. Wanker', 'Yes, Mr Wanker', 'No, Mr Wanker'

– and so on. And then they introduced his wife – Mrs Wanker...

No one checked the content of this usually innocuous sitcom when it arrived in the UK and it was broadcast quite happily here in a Saturday teatime slot... One can just see distressed parents racing for the 'off' button...

No fewer than 95 episodes of *Mork and Mindy* were made. Guess which one of the 95 they chose to adapt into a children's picture book. Apparently, it now fetches rather high prices on eBay – if you can find it at all.

Footnote: Another American sitcom also included Wankers amongst its supporting cast. In *Married... with Children*, the long-suffering Al Bundy's in-laws were Mr and Mrs Wanker.

Naff Swearing

The phrase 'Naff off', much beloved of Ronnie Barker's character Fletcher in *Porridge* (as in 'Naff off Godber, you nirk'), was far less innocent than the BBC executives running the show knew at the time. *Naff* is actually Australian slang for *Nasty as Fuck.* It has also been adopted by the gay community as an abusive term for straight men. It's an acronym for Not A Fucking Fairy.

In the same way, BBC executives seemed quite oblivious to what the crew of *Red Dwarf* actually meant when they said 'Smeg' and 'Smeg off' – which they did frequently. Perhaps they thought it was some made up futuristic slang. It is, of course a diminution of smegma, the soapy secretion that accumulates under the foreskin – or what we lesser-educated people might term knob cheese... A Mrs Smegma of Belmont once appeared on an episode of *Monty Python's Flying Circus* and no-one raised an eyebrow... N.B. the word smegma actually derives from the Greek word meaning 'soap'.

(Incidentally, there's also an American experimental free-jazz group called Smegma. Wonder if they sell many T-shirts on tour...)

Oriental Wisdom

In China, Internet cafés are referred to as *wang-kas.*

This is very astute on the part of the Chinese. They obviously know their clientele. As anyone who has access to the Internet knows, providing masturbatory fodder is its primary purpose — after giving Eastern Europeans an easy means of accessing your private online bank account, that is.

Sweary Mary

A new playground rhyme recently discovered
by *The Sunday Times* went:

'Mary, Mary, quite contrary.
How does your garden grow?
I live in a flat,
You stupid prat.
So how the fuck should I know?'

Queen Victoria and Cock

The use of the word cock to describe the penis was considered quite acceptable until Queen Victoria made a particular point to ban the word from her court. After which polite society naturally followed suit.

Why she hated the word so much is not known, given that she was rather partial to the penis, what with all the sprogs she had and her fling with commoner John Brown.

Russian Anti-Swearing Crackdown

We all know how Russia still likes the occasional good old-fashioned crackdown on things – just to keep its hand in the repression business...

Since July 2004, authorities in the Belgorod region of Russia have declared war on swearing. Anyone heard uttering obscene words in public faces a stiff fine (typically around an average week's wages). Offenders who refuse to pay can be charged with hooliganism and jailed for up to two weeks.

In under three months police have fined over two and a half thousand people – hardly surprising when you consider they get to personally pocket a third of the fine. In fact, the scheme has proved so popular amongst local policemen that they have been encouraging people to shop their friends and neighbours if they hear them cussing. Furthermore, an anti-swearing poster with the slogan, 'Your tongue is your enemy. Swearing is the death of your soul' displayed in the area shows a man whose tongue has been cut off with a pair of shears.

'The campaign is working,' said local official Pavel Bespalenko 'We have already noticed people swearing less. We should remove from their heads the idea that it's cool to swear. They must learn to be ashamed to use vulgar language.'

Other Russian regions are now considering following suit.

Hell Hath No Fury like a Gay Man Scorned

Outraged by the anti-homosexual rhetoric spouted by United States Senator Rick Santorum, gay men started to use the term Santorum to refer to that particularly revolting mixture of lubricant and faecal matter that can result after a messy bout of gay anal sex.

Swearing and Hollywood

It's probably a question that's perplexed you for years. Which Hollywood movie contains the most swear words? Here's a clue – it's actually a cartoon – and no, it isn't *Bambi*.

The record for obscenities in one feature film was originally held by Al Pacino's *Scarface*. (The film's most famous line, 'Say hello to my little friend...' wasn't one of them, as Al was referring to a bloody big gun at the time and not his winky). That film boasted 204 swear words. Then, along came *Goodfellas* with a tally of 246 obscenities – only to have its crown lifted in 1994 by *Pulp Fiction*, which racked up an impressive 257 dirty words.

But the reigning champion is none other than *South Park – Bigger, Longer & Uncut*, blowing away all opposition in 1999 with an incredible 399 obscenities (not to mention a further 128 'offensive gestures'). It remains unbeaten to this day.

Incredibly the film received an Oscar nomination for one of its songs – the fairly innocuous 'Blame Canada'. This was probably because the Academy could not possibly nominate the film's truly outstanding song, 'Uncle Fucka'. Originally entitled 'Muthafucka', the song uses the word fuck over 30 times in under three minutes. An average line goes something like, 'You're a cock-sucking, arse-licking Uncle Fucka' and ends with a synchronised burst of prolonged flatulence and the cry of 'Suck my balls!'.

Rude (Real) Product Names

Bum crisps

(Spain)

The Ikea Fartfull workbench

(Sweden)

The Ikea Beslut chair

(Sweden)

The Ikea Femmen Vag shower curtain

(Sweden)

The Ikea Kunti wall shelf range

(Sweden)

Bra milk

(Sweden)

Plopp chocolate

(Sweden)

Barf washing powder

(Poland)

SuperPiss antifreeze

(Finland)

Incidentally, in America, a company called Mama Rosa's do a pizza range called 'Bite my Slice'.

FOOTNOTE: Honorary mentions must also go to VAG (Volkswagen Audi Group) and Smeg, well-known names in our own country.

And you thought Shakespeare was boring?

Wrong. Once in a while, the great bard was capable of a cracking filthy double entendre. Check out Act 3, Scene 2 of *Hamlet*, which contains a rather obvious play on the word cunt:

Hamlet: Lady, shall I lie in your lap?
Ophelia: No, my lord.
Hamlet: I mean, my head upon your lap?
Ophelia: Ay, my lord.
Hamlet: Do you think I mean country matters?
Ophelia: I think nothing, my lord.
Hamlet: That's a fair thought to lie between maids' legs.

The Cunt Club

What on earth is The Cunt Club? Is it a loose collective term for all those who voted for George Galloway at the last election? Is it like the Freemasons, with membership being restricted to BBC executives? Is it Manchester United?

In fact, The Cunt Club is an official organisation at Wesleyan University, whose sole aim is to reclaim the word for women. Their philosophy is related to Germaine Greer's idea of 'Cunt Power' (this has nothing to do with superheroes or superpowers).

Reclaiming the word during Eve Ensler's one-woman feminist play *The Vagina Monologues* takes a very unusual form of crowd participation with audiences sometimes being encouraged to stand up and chant 'Cunt! Cunt! Cunt! Cunt!' over and over again (close your eyes and you could almost be at a Will Young concert...)

Audiences have also been requested to end the evening with a rousing singalong of 'Cunt Cunt Cunt Cunt' to the tune of 'Frére Jacques'.

All together now...

The *Guardian* makes history

Which national newspaper claims to be the first in the world to use the word cunt on its front page? None other than our very own *Guardian*.

After the notorious World Cup bust-up between Republic of Ireland manager Mick McCarthy and team captain Roy Keane in 2002, the *Guardian* openly quoted Keane as saying 'You're not even Irish, you English cunt.'

For those interested in football trivia and swearing, *Guardian* journalist Paul Kelso quotes Keane's full rousing speech as 'You were a crap player and you are a crap manager. The only reason I have any dealings with you is that somehow you are the manager of my country and you're not even Irish, you English cunt. You can stick it up your bollocks... you were a cunt in 1994, again in 1998 and you're even more of a cunt now – and you ain't even Irish.'

(Rude) Words of Wisdom

'After dinner I always like to have the four Cs: Champagne, cigars, cognac and cunt.'

Singer Tom Jones

The Queen Classic That Never Was

Freddie Mercury's original title for the Queen song 'Life is Real' was 'Cunt Stains on my Pillow' (like he'd know about that...).

Incidentally, there's no truth in the persistent rumour that Paul McCartney's working title for 'Yesterday' was 'Suck my Cock'. It was actually (and this is 100% true), 'Scrambled Egg'. Go figure.

The Joke With the Most Swear Words – Official!

A man walks into the swankiest restaurant in town and says to the waiter, 'Where's your motherfucking, cock-sucking arsewipe of a manager, you fucking poncy cunt?'

Shocked, the waiter replies, 'Please moderate your language, sir. I shall summon the manager immediately.' And he leaves.

So, the manager finishes what he's doing and hurries in. The man turns to him and says, 'Are you the fucking syphilitic cunt-rag who runs this shithole place?'

'Yes,' replies the manager, 'and please – there's no need for that sort of language...'

'Fuck off, cum stain!' replies the man. 'And where's your fucking piano then?'

'What?' says the manager.

'Are you fucking deaf as well as fucking stupid you dozy cunt? Where's your fucking piano then?'

'Oh,' says the manager, 'You've come about the pianist job...' Nervously, he shows the man to the restaurant's grand piano and asks him, 'Can you play any Blues?'

'Fuck me! Of course I fucking can. Piece of piss,' declares the man, as he sits down and plays the most stunning and inspired piece of original honky-tonk that the manager has ever heard.

Despite his reservations about the man, the manager tells him that that was the best Blues playing he'd ever heard and asks what the song was called.

'"I Want to Fuck your Fucking Wife up the Shitter on your King-Sized Bed but the Springs Keep Hurting my Bell end"', replies the man.

The manager hurriedly changes the subject and asks him if he can play any Jazz. Again, the man produces the most original and haunting jazz piece the manager has ever heard. It virtually reduces him to tears. 'Magnificent!' he cries. 'What's it called?'

'"I Wanked off in Your Hair you Crack Whore and There's Still Spunk in it"', replies the man.

Rather perplexed, the manager asks the man if he knows any romantic ballads. Once again, the man plays an utterly captivating and moving song. The manager reluctantly forces himself to ask what it is called...

'"As I Fuck You at Midnight with the Starlight Shining off your Cunt"', the man declares.

The manager thinks for a minute, unsure what to do. He's deeply worried by the man's language, given the class of the establishment, but – on the other hand – the man is undoubtedly a musical genius. Eventually, he offers him the pianist's job on the strict condition that he doesn't introduce any of his songs or talk to any customers.

So things go really well for the first few weeks. Crowds hear about the pianist and start flocking to the restaurant to hear the man play. Business is booming. And one night, in walks this knockout blonde and sits down at the table nearest the piano. She's wearing a dress that's virtually see-through and she's sitting there looking at him with her legs apart and he can see she's wearing no underwear. What's worse, she's sucking suggestively on asparagus shoots and the liquid butter is dripping down her chin.

This is all too much for the man. He finishes up the tune he is playing, rushes to the toilets and furiously starts to jerk himself off. Then he hears the manager's voice calling, 'Where's the bloody pianist?'

The man just has time to finish himself off, quickly re-arrange his clothing and run back to the piano to continue playing. Then the blonde he is so infatuated with leans forward and whispers in his ear, 'Do you know your cock and balls are hanging out off your trouser flies and dripping spunk on your shoes?'

'Know it?' the man replies, 'I fucking wrote it!'

Great Places to Swear – the football terraces

Sung by Manchester United fans to taunt their arch rivals City:

If I had the wings of a sparrow, If I had the arse of a crow,
I'd fly over Maine Road tomorrow,
And shit on the bastards below, below,
Shit on, shit on,
Shit on the bastards below, below,
Shit on, shit on,
Shit on the bastards below.

You're the shit of Manchester,

You're the shit of Manchester.

The Man City riposte. ('Munich' refers to the Munich Air Disaster in which eight Manchester United players lost their lives):

(To the tune of 'My Old Man Said Follow the Van')

My old man said, 'Be a Munich fan',
I said, 'Fuck off bollocks you're a cunt,
I'd rather fuck a bucket with a large hole in it,
Than be a Munich fan for a single minute',
I fucked it, I fucked it,
I fucked and I fucked,
I fucked it till I couldn't fuck no more,
And I got more out of fucking that bucket,
Than seeing United score.

Leeds United's greeting to a visiting Manchester United:

Manchester wank wank wank!

Manchester wank wank wank!

Manchester wank wank wank!

Manchester United are not popular at Everton either:

Oh Manchester,
Oh Manchester,
Is full of shit,
Is full of shit.
It's full of shit, shit and more shit.
Oh Manchester is full of shit.

Sorry – on lawyers' advice we had to leave out all those chants about Victoria Beckham which are so popular throughout the land. Anyway, we're sure he isn't and we're sure she doesn't.

Seven Words You Can Never Say on Television

In 1978 the US Supreme Court ruled that the following words were not permitted to be broadcast during the day:

Shit

Piss

Fuck

Cunt

Cocksucker
Motherfucker
and... Tits

They were upholding a US Federal Communications Commission ruling about a 1973 broadcast by comedian George Carlin. His performance was called, appropriately enough, 'Seven Words You Can Never Say On Television'. (Since the ruling, Carlin's broadcast has been shown repeatedly on TV).

In 2002, Andrea Wills, the BBC's chief advisor on editorial policy, stated that, 'In research, 50% or more people said the words that should never be broadcast are cunt, motherfucker, nigger, Paki and spastic. Young women also don't like whore, slag and twat'.

But fuck wasn't on the list.

23 Brazen and Knavish Elizabethan Curses

Back in Shakespeare's time they didn't call someone a 'fucking wanker' or a 'worthless cunt' – they used far richer language in their curses...

1. Thou lumpish sour-faced pumpion!

2. Thou clouted fly-bitten malt-worm!

3. Thou fawning unchin-snouted rudesby!

4. Thou bootless pus-sore rabbit-sucker!

5. Thou reeky spur-galled minnow!

6. Thou spleeny milk-livered cutpurse!

7. Thou goatish sour-faced haggard!

8. Thou purpled unchin-snouted vassal!

9. Thou surly raw-boned death-token!

10. Thou froward slack-mouthed younker!

11. Thou weedy bunched-backed minimus!

12. Thou quailing fat-kidneyed swine hound!

13. Thou whoreson tickle-brained ratsbane!

14. Thou yeasty ill-breeding malignancy!

15. Thou goatish rough-hewn strumpet!

16. Thou spongy fat-kidneyed jolthead!

17. Thou clouted milk-livered boar-pig!

18. Thou lewd bunched-backed moldwarp!

19. Thou spleeny ill-nurtured hugger-mugger!

20. Thou clouted pottle-deep whey-face!

21. Thou loggerheaded knotty-pated vassal!

22. Thou impertinent fat-kidneyed apple-john!

23. Thou queasy bat-fowling lewdster!

Great Instances of Royalty Swearing

In 1900 an anarchist shot Prince Edward, the Prince of Wales while he was waiting for a train at Brussels railway station. After feeling a sharp pain the Prince turned to his aides and exclaimed, 'Fuck it. I've taken a bullet!'

In 1982 Princess Anne told a group of paparazzi to 'Naff off' as they photographed her falling from her horse and getting soaked at the Badminton Horse Trials.

In 1997 Prince Philip insulted a Cambridge University car park attendant who failed to recognise him by calling him a 'Bloody silly fool!'

In 2005 Prince Charles' whispered remarks to his sons during a photo call at the Klosters ski resort were picked up by reporters' microphones. He was clearly heard to say, 'Bloody people. I can't bear that man. He's so awful, he really is.' The Prince was referring to journalists in general and the BBC's royal correspondent, Nicholas Witchell, in particular. Later Paddy Harverson, the Prince's communication's secretary, said Prince Charles' comments were regretted.

18 Movies with the word fuck in the title

1. I Gonna Fuck You Back To The Stone Age
2. In God We Fuck
3. The Internet Fuck
4. Mod Fuck Explosion
5. Fuck Norge
6. Fuck: The Movie
7. Fuck Coke

The Songs of Anal Cunt

Q: Which punk/heavy metal crossover group has covered the theme tune to 'Hungry, Hungry Hippos' and the Bee Gees 'Stayin' Alive', shared a set with the band Vaginal Jesus, released songs titled 'You're A Fucking Cunt' and 'You Robbed A Sperm Bank Because You're A Cum Guzzling Fag' and were once described as 'one of the most offensive and musically challenging bands to ever produce music'?

A: It could only be Anal Cunt (or AC as they are sometimes known). Infamous for their short 'grindcore' songs with some of the most offensive titles in music history,

Anal Cunt began in 1988 as a 'sonic experiment', describing themselves as the 'most non-musical band in the world'. As you can imagine, the band's name alone has caused them to have many distribution problems.

The following are just some of their songs:

1. I Sent Concentration Camp Footage To America's Funniest Home Videos

2. The Only Reason Why Men Talk To You Is Because They Want To Get Laid

3. You Stupid Fuckin' Cunts

4. I Snuck a Retard Into A Sperm Bank

5. Hitler Was A Sensitive Man

6. You're Pregnant So I Kicked You In the Stomach

7. I Made Your Kid Get AIDS So You Could Watch It Die

8. I Fucked Your Wife

9. Everyone In Anal Cunt Is Dumb

10. I Convinced You To Beat Your Wife On A Daily Basis

11. I Got Athletes Foot Showering At Mike's

12. You Were Too Ugly To Rape, So I Just Beat The Shit Out Of You

13. I Just Saw The Gayest Guy On Earth

14. I Lit Your Baby On Fire

15. Windchimes Are Gay

16. I Sent A Thank You Card To The Guy That Raped You

17. I Sold Your Dog To A Chinese Restaurant

18. Internet Is Gay

19. I Intentionally Ran Over Your Dog

20. Phyllis Is An Old Annoying Cunt

21. You're A Fucking Cunt

22. Recycling Is Gay

23. Technology is Gay

24. The Word Homophobic Is Gay

25. Van Full Of Retards

26. You Got Date Raped

27. Jack Kevorkian Is Cool

28. I Got An Office Job
For The Sole Purpose Of
Sexually Harassing Women

29. I Like Drugs And
Child Abuse

30. You Rollerblading
Faggot

31. Pottery's Gay

32. You're Gay

33.You're Old (Fuck You)

Lewd Limerick

There was a young man from Nantucket

Took a pig in a forest to fuck it

Said the pig with a grunt

'Stay away from my cunt

Come around to the front and I'll suck it.'

A Short History of Swearing in Entertainment

1965: Appearing on the programme *BBC3*, a late-night satirical review on BBC television, the author and drama critic Kenneth Tynan became the first man to say 'fuck' on TV. (He actually said, 'I doubt if there are any rational people to whom the word fuck would be particularly diabolical, revolting or totally forbidden.') The BBC issued a formal apology and Mrs Mary Whitehouse, guardian of the nation's morals, wrote to the Queen suggesting that Tynan 'ought to have his bottom spanked'.

1967: An episode of the sitcom *Til Death Us Do Part* featured 44 uses of the word 'bloody'. Mary Whitehouse stated that this 'was the end of civilisation as we know it'.

1976: Bill Grundy was sacked as presenter of Thames Televisions' *Today* programme and disappeared into obscurity after goading the Sex Pistols to say 'dirty fucker' and 'fucking rotter' on live television.

1983: Musician and presenter Jools Holland let slip the phrase 'groovy fuckers' during a live trailer for Tyne Tees television's *The Tube* and was suspended for six weeks.

1998: The first use of the word 'cunt' in a TV drama was in *Mosley*, a four part Channel Four series about the rise and fall of the British Fascist leader, Sir Oswald Mosley.

Alternatives for Motherfucker

If you ever get bored of using the word motherfucker (and let's face it, it could happen), but still want to express this expression of Oedipal love, then why not use one of these American alternatives:

Mama-huncher

Mama-jabber

Mammy-dodger

Mammy-jammer
Mammy-rammer
Maryland Farmer
Mo dicker
Mofo / Mo fo
Mofuck
Mother-flicker
Mother-flunker
Mother-fouler
Mother-grabber
Mother-hubba
Mother-hugger
Mother-humper

Mother-jiver
Motherlover
Motheroo
Mother-rubba
Mother-sucker
Muddy funster
Mudfucker
Muhfukkuh

P.S. The actual origin of the word motherfucker has nothing to do with Freud. The word was apparently coined by African slaves in the US to describe the slave owners who had raped the slaves' mothers.

Words for Wankers

No, not the former name of Tears For Fears (although it would be apt). Try these euphemisms when you need a way to describe some tosser...

Bone stroker

Fuck-fist

Knob jockey

Knob-shiner

Meat beater

Milkman

Monkey spanker
Pud puller
Salami slapper
Spankhead
Tossprick
Virtuoso of the skin flute
Wank-bag
Whacker
Wrist

Well, Fug Me!

In his book *The Naked and the Dead* (1948), author Norman Mailer was pressurised to use the word 'fug' in place of the four letter expletive. Later, when Dorothy Parker met the young novelist at a literary party, she told him, 'So you're the young man who can't spell "fuck".'

Free Speech

During anti-Milosevic demonstrations, Serbian students belonging to Otpor, the resistance movement, shouted an insult that reflected Milosevic's fascination with Communist China: '*Mars v materinu Kinu*' which means 'We march on your mother's Chinese cunt' (we're sure it means a lot more if you're Serbian).

At protest marches the same group would yell, '*Idem peske, jebem bez greske!*' declaring 'I'm going on foot, fuck you with no mistake!'

The Difference between Curses and Swear Words

Professor Dr Nedeljko Bogdanoviç, a man who has spent several years of his life studying swearing in Serbia (there's obviously not much on TV), explained the difference between curses and swearing: 'The first merely degrades, while the second is malicious. For example, a curse would be "May your plum tree never grow plums!" while in the same situation, swearing would be "Fuck you AND your plums!"'

About Face

The British verify nudity from the front, as in saying someone is 'bollock naked' while the Americans verify it from behind, as in 'butt naked'. No one knows why...

C.U.N.T.S

There are a few urban legends about school names that were completely and utterly inoffensive until they were abbreviated. No one has verified that these stories are true, but we wish they were...

Cambridge University New Testament Society

City University, Newcastle upon Tyne
(the former name of Newcastle Polytechnic)

Sheffield Hallam Institute
of Technology

Friends University of
Central Kansas

Peterborough Institute for
Social Sciences

Wolverhampton Academy
New College

Bulgarian Buggerers

The word 'bugger' derives from Bulgaria and a group of people known as the Bogomils. These were originally a Christian sect who were accused of heresy by taking part in mass buggery sessions.

N.B. According to Section Twelve of the UK 1956 Sexual Offences Act, buggery is sexual intercourse between males or between male and female in an 'unnatural manner', or between male or female with an animal in any manner whatsoever.

So now you know.

Charles Dickens – the Naughty Bits

The rudest name in classical literature is probably to be found in Charles Dickens' otherwise rather tame *The Old Curiosity Shop.* Famed for his unusual character names, Dickens really outdid himself when he came up with Dick Swiveller. (His other classic rude name was, of course, Master (Charlie) Bates from *Oliver Twist.*)

Today, over 160 years later, we can still share in a couple of Charlie's dirty little jokes. However, how many of the rest of his weird character names were actually based on now-forgotten Victorian swear words? Did the streets of Victorian England once ring with such phrases as:

'Phew! Prithee good sirs, who's just dropped *a chuzzlewit*?'

'Hang on a mo, Guv'nor; I'm just having one off the *Oliver Twist*...'

'A strange chap indeed. If you ask me, he's one of them *Wackford Squeers*'

'I cannot sit comfortably on account of my inflamed *Quilps*'

'He was a common *Tappertit*, alarming many respectable women with his quick hands...'

'I don't mean to boast luv, but me old *Micawber* is the toast of all East Ham'

'Look at the *Nubbles* on her!'

'Her *Little Dorrit* had seen many visitors in its time yet still was in prime condition and indeed was considered something of a *Jerry Cruncher* amongst the cogniscenti of such things.'

'Having expended his *Major Bagstock* somewhat earlier alone in the First Class carriage, his spirits were now low. Joylessly and with less than great expectations he nevertheless pulled out his *Wopsle* and *pumblechooked* until he had his *Podsnap* and his *herbert pocket* was spent...'

'The kick caught him squarely in his *noggs*.'

'I must make my way home swiftly, for fear that I have a case of the *Trotty Vecks* coming on and I am not sure how long I can clench my *Gamp* for before the *Traddles* are truly upon me and a *Turveydrop* becomes imminent.'

'Alas, he was tired and all he could present before his good lady wife was a *Dombey*. How she longed for a *MacStinger*, a true *Tulkinghorn* to satisfy her *Miff* and – dare she even think such a thing – her *Creackle*. Alas, there would be no *gradgrind* for her tonight. Perhaps if I give him a *Princess Puffer*, she thought.'

'He was famed for his *Dick Datchery*, despite only possessing a meagre *Skimpole*.'

'Her *Little Nell* had a bad dose of the *Skettles*.'

The Flexibility of Fuck

Rarely has a word been so flexible in use. The word fuck can be used in many grammatical ways, for example:

A TRANSITIVE VERB: e.g. 'Charles fucks Camilla'

A PASSIVE VERB: e.g. 'Camilla was fucked by Charles'

AN ADJECTIVE: e.g. 'Charles is talking a load of fucking crap'

AN ADVERB: e.g. 'Camilla talks too fucking much'

A NOUN: e.g. 'I don't give a fuck about the Royal Family'

AS PART OF A WORD: e.g. 'abso-fucking-lutely' or 'in-fucking-credible'

AS ALMOST EVERY WORD IN THE SENTENCE: e.g. 'Royalty? Fuck the fucking fuckers.'

As you can see in these examples, there are few words as versatile as 'fuck':

Dismay:
'Fuck it!'

Inquiry:
'Who the fuck does she think he is?'

Disbelief:
'Unfuckingbelievable!'

Retaliation:
'Shove it up your fucking ass.'

Surprise:
'Fuck me!'

Dissatisfaction:
'I don't like what the fuck is going on here.'

Incompetence:
'He's such a fuck-up.'

Ignorance:
'Fucked if I know.'

Displeasure:
'What the fuck is going on here?'

Trouble:
'I guess I'm really fucked now.'

Aggression:
'Don't fuck with me mister!'

Difficulty:
'I don't understand what I should fucking do.'

Greetings:
'How the fuck are you?'

Confusion:
'What the fuck...?'

Exasperation:
'For fuck's sake.'

Fraud:
'I got fucked over by those con men.'

Enjoyment:
'This is fucking great.'

Hostility:
'I'm going to smash your fucking face in.'

Disorientation:
'Where the fuck are we?'

Suspicion:
'What the fuck are you doing?'

Contempt:
'Fuck you and your family!'

Useful Yiddish Swear Words

Tochus leker

Arse licker

Schmuck

Prick

Putz

Prick

Kurva

Whore

Dreck

Shit

Shtup

To fuck

Tochus

Arse

Putznasher

Prick sucker

Schlemiel

Retard

Pierick

Cunt

Gay k'ken in yam

Go shit in the ocean

Faygala
Faggot

Tuches arine
Up your arse

Kish mine tuches
Kiss my arse

Shtup ir
Fuck you

Gay k' ken oyf der vant
Go shit on the wall

Shtik drek
Piece of shit

Kucker
Shit head

Sixteenth-century Fuck

One of the earliest written uses of the word 'fuck' appears in a poem written around the year 1500 called 'Flen flyys'. The poem takes its title from the first line 'Flen, flyss and freris' meaning 'Fleas, Flies and Friars', and satirises the Carmelite monks of Cambridge.

The poem, written in a mix of Latin and English, contains the line: '*Non sunt in celi quia fuccant uuiuys of heli.*'

This translates as: 'They [the monks] are not in heaven because they fuck the wives of Ely' [the town near Cambridge].

Offensive?
Fuck Off!

Charles Jones, Professor of English Language at Edinburgh University, gave evidence in 2001 that helped Kenneth Kinnaird of Glasgow successfully appeal against a breach of the peace conviction. Kinnaird had been arrested after telling an Edinburgh traffic policeman to 'Fuck off'. Lord Prosser, presiding, agreed with Professor Jones that Kinnaird, 43, was only using the 'language of his generation'.

Jones told the court, 'For many working-class men, fuck seems to me hardly countable as an explitive. Rather it is used as a reinforcing adverb: "It's fucking cold/hot/terrible" or whatever. Some purists argue that this shows an inability on the part of these speakers to use (or even to have) more sophisticated vocabulary, but I doubt this. In my view, nothing is regrettable in linguistic usage.'

In the same year, the *Church Times*, the 138-year-old official newspaper of the Church of England, printed the word fuck without deleting any of the letters. The word occurred in an article about the hostility exhibited toward some nuns, such as the sister who had a drunken lout scream in her face, 'Fucking nun!' Her reported response was, 'I can be one or the other, but not both.' The *Church Times*' editor said he spelled the word out in full because it's 'not an uncommon word these days, even in church circles.'

These two cases are actually nothing new. Ten years earlier in 1991, Lord Rees-Mogg, chairman of the Broadcasting Standards Council, claimed that the word fuck was 'rapidly losing its power to shock and is becoming steadily and rapidly drained of force'. His proof included the fact that 'the F-word is now used in private conversations by professors'.

Taking the Piss

The only profanity used in the Bible is 'piss', which appears in the King James version in the following books:

2 Kings 9:8

2 Kings 18:27

Isaiah 36:12

1 Samuel 25:22

1 Samuel 25:34

1 Kings 14:10

1 Kings 16:11

1 Kings 21:21

Many modern translations have changed the word to urine or urinate.

Wanker: The North/South Divide

According to a recent study, the word 'wanker' was viewed as being more severe by a greater number of people in the Midlands and North than in the South of England (45% vs. 37%). Does this mean there are more wankers in the Midlands / North or they're more self-conscious? You make up your own mind...

Vietnamese Names

Common Vietnamese first names are Phuc and Bich. It makes you glad you were christened Tristram.

F.U.C.K. in the U.S.S.R

Until 1990 the Russian words for penis, cunt, fuck and whore were prohibited in magazines and newspapers in Russia and even today they remain banned on TV and in the movies. The situation is similar in Japan where even the words for vagina and penis are usually censored when appearing in print by replacing the central character of each word with an 'O' symbol.

Setting an Example

In June 2004 Vice President Dick Cheney, serving in his role as President of the Senate, appeared in the chamber for a photo session. A chance meeting with Senator Patrick J. Leahy of Vermont grew into an animated argument about Cheney's ties to Halliburton Co., an international energy services corporation. The exchange ended when Cheney offered the Senator some sage – but anatomically impossible – advice, when he said, 'Fuck yourself!'

His comment was printed in full, without asterisks, in the *Washington Post*. After the heated conversation Leahy's spokesman,

David Carle, commented that, 'The Vice President seemed to be taking personally the criticism that Senator Leahy and others have levelled against Halliburton's sole-source contracts in Iraq.' As for Cheney, well his office did not deny that he had uttered this phrase.

By chance, Cheney's remark came on the same day that the Senate passed legislation described as the Defense of Decency Act.

More Literary Filth from Dickens

'She touched his organ, and from that bright epoch, even it, the old companion of his happiest hours, incapable as he had thought of elevation, began a new and deified existence.'

from *Martin Chuzzlewit* by Charles Dickens.

The British Empire's Second Greatest Gift to the World

According to author Niall Ferguson, on the eve that South Yemen received its independence, the last British governor there hosted a dinner party attended by Denis Healey, then the Minister for Defence.

As the Union Jack was about to be lowered over the capital of Aden for the final time, the governor turned to Healey and said, 'You know, Minister, I believe that in the long view of history, the British Empire will be remembered only for two things.'

Healey asked the Governor with interest what these were, to which the governor replied, matter-of-factly, 'The game of football. And the expression "fuck off".'

What a Crock!

Did you ever wonder where the word 'shit' comes from? (We did.)

When certain types of manure used to be transported by ship, care had to be taken not to allow this cargo to come into contact with any salt water. This caused the manure to ferment, giving off large quantities of methane gas in the process. This methane would build-up in confined spaces, like below decks, and a careless sailor with a lantern could accidentally ignite it – causing a massive explosion. Several ships were destroyed in this manner before the cause of the accidents was discovered.

After that, bundles of manure where always stamped with the letters S.H.I.T on them which stood for 'Ship High In Transit', i.e. high enough off the lower decks so that any water that came into the hold would not touch this volatile cargo.

Actually, that's a load of crap and is just an urban myth.

The word 'shit' actually derives from the Old English scite and the Middle Low German schite, both meaning 'dung', and the Old English noun scitte, meaning 'diarrhoea'. The word appears in written works both as a noun and as a verb as far back as the fourteenth century.

What They Say... And What They Really Mean

Possibly due to years of being the victims of oppressive state regimes, the Chileans have developed two unique phrases that they probably use as they are being bundled into the back of an unmarked police car, or having electrodes strapped to their genitals.

Ojo de pollo

What it means literally: **Chicken's eye**
What it really means: **Puckering anus**

Boca de mono

What it means literally: **Monkey's mouth**
What it really means: **Cunt**

It's What Freedom of Speech is all About...

All was going well at the December 2004 Spirit of Liberty Celebration, held in honour of those individuals who have made outstanding contributions to advancing the values and principles of freedom of religion, tolerance, civic responsibility, and equal opportunity. Actors Alec Baldwin and Susan Sarandon delivered fine, emotive speeches accepting their Defender of Democracy awards and then comedian Chevy Chase took to the stage one last time to really say what was on his mind calling the newly re-elected President Bush a 'dumb fuck', adding for good measure, 'I'm no fucking clown either. This guy started a jihad.' Toning down his language Chase finished his speech by saying, 'This guy in office is an uneducated, real lying schmuck . . . and we still couldn't beat him with a bore like Kerry.'

The event's organisers, People for the American Way, distanced itself from the actor's rant. Their president, Ralph Neas said, 'Chevy Chase's improvised remarks caught everyone off guard, and were inappropriate and offensive. It was not what I would have said, and certainly not the language People for the American Way would ever use in discussing any president of the United States.'

Your Mother's Smelly Cunt

and other useful international sign language

Traditionally, if someone gives you the finger or makes a V-sign you instantly recognise the fact that they are telling you to 'fuck off!' However, there are many national versions of these gestures that you might not be as familiar with. With some it is obvious what the message is. Others are not so clear and you might take a particular gesture as being a quaint local greeting rather than a gesture that questions your mother's hygiene.

Gesture 1
'The forearm jerk'

Description:

One hand slapped to the inner elbow, and that arm raised with a fist

Location:

France, Southern Europe, some part of the Middle East

What it means:

This gesture originated in France where it is known as 'the arm of honour'. The combination of a fist and the representation of a giant erect penis says 'fuck off' in a far stronger way than the puny middle-finger or V-sign. For extra effect, the hand should strike the inner elbow area with a loud slapping sound; the louder the sound, the stronger the insult.

Gesture 2
'The thumbs-up'

Description:

A thumb thrusted-up as high as possible

Location:

Parts of Italy and Greece, Nigeria, Iran and Afghanistan

What it means:

A thrusted thumb can signify a sign of approval or 'good luck' but in these countries, if the gesture is made violently, with an accompanied grimaced facial expression, it is a gross insult, especially if it accompanied by a sweep of the arms. In this case it means 'Up yours' or literally, 'sit on my prick'. In Sardinia the gesture is considered extremely obscene and many hitchhikers hoping to be given a lift by a large lorry are advised to think of an alternative signal for drivers.

Gesture 3
'The open palm'

Description:

An open palm being thrust towards someone

Location:

Greece and parts of North Africa

What it means:

In Greece this gesture is called 'moutza' and it means 'eat shit!'. The sign refers to the ancient practice of villagers thrusting shit in the faces of chained criminals paraded around town. In modern Greece, any motion where the palm is held outwards is deemed offensive and in southern Greece, people wave good-bye instead with the palm facing inwards. (Fucking idiots.)

Gesture 4
'Finger insertion'

Description:

The middle finger is poked into the other hand which is making a fist.

Location:

France

What it means:

This is a polite way (or as polite as you can actually be) of saying "You take it up the arse." This gesture doesn't have the same impact of the 'arm of honour' but it's still very insulting.

Gesture 5
'The four finger thrust'

Description:

Four fingers being thrust towards someone

Location:

Japan

What it means:

The Japanese don't like lots of people, but one group they really hate are the Koreans. They call them "animals" by thrusting four fingers of one hand into the recipient's face. (OK, calling someone an 'animal' isn't that a big deal to us, but if you're Korean, you'd be absofuckinglutely livid.)

Gesture 6
'Upthrust palm and finger curl'

Description:

Fingers curled into the palm, and the palm thrust outwards

Location:

Chile

What it means:

Known as 'Concha de tu madre', (or just 'Concha' for short'), the phrase literally means 'Your mother's shell' – which is not an insult in its own right. However, the gesture has the real meaning of 'Your mother's smelly cunt' and is used as an alternative to giving the finger.

Yes Lord, We Will Shit With You

OK, it's not as well known as 'All Things Bright & Beautiful' or 'He Who Would Valiant Be' but this is an album from the Alabama-based group Supreme Dispassion, a group whose music has been described as 'jazz rock blasphemy'.

Tracks include 'Pray That You Do Not Shit Blood', 'Painting The Scrotum With Lamb's Blood', 'Painting With Horse Menstruation' and 'Partial Birth Abortion Baby Jesus'. One review of the album said, 'The short, demented, anthem-like songs have a ProgRock quality' and that 'the bass and guitar work is intricate'.

Tracks released on other albums include 'Christmas Tree Monster Cock', 'A Dove Flew Out Of A Colostomy', 'Big Bowel Movement In The Little Town Of Bethlehem' and 'This Prayer Cloth Is A Jack Off Rag'. In the track 'Catholics Surround Me' you'll hear the priceless lyric, 'I disapprove of the Vatican touching my butt-hole' – and you won't find that on a Keane album. Well not unless you play it backwards.

N.B. Another US group which constantly upsets the moral majority is The Crucifucks.

This is what we think of NATO

A common Serbian anti-NATO slogan was *'Klintone, mozes da nam pusis, Sirak nabijem ti Ajfelovu kulu u dupe, Olbrajtovo, kurvo stara.'* This translated as 'Clinton, you can give us a blow job, Chirac, I'll stuff the Eiffel Tower up your arse, Albright, old bitch.'

Swearing OK at Work— or is it?

In 1997, Judge Charles Schaefer of the town of Superior in Wisconsin, denied unemployment benefits to a woman who resigned from her job at a Kentucky Fried Chicken restaurant. The woman said she left because of the amount of vile language in the workplace. Judge Schaefer ruled that, 'The use of vulgar and obscene language can promote group solidarity.'

However, more recently a number of US companies have introduced language-control policies in order to prevent, or at least reduce, the use of swearing in the workplace. Known as 'anti-cussing' policies, these controls have been working and are creating better working conditions, especially where women are involved in manufacturing facilities. These environments are rife with 'inappropriate language', which the anti-cussing policies define as 'unwanted, deliberate, repeated, unsolicited profanity, cussing, swearing, vulgar, insulting, abusive or crude language'.

Profanity Delays – Bunch of Arse?

Imagine interviewing Ozzy Osborne (or any of the Osborne clan) on live radio. It's just asking for trouble. Radio stations often use a 'profanity delay system', when interviewing controversial guests or hosting live phone-ins. This equipment delays the broadcast signal so that the presenter or engineer can bleep-out any offensive words or libellous comments, or play a jingle over them, before they go out on air.

One of the most sophisticated profanity delay systems on the market goes by the name (and we're not kidding) of Arse! The manufacturer's web site (www.profanitydelay.com) shows ARSE! in use and lists 'reasons why you will love ARSE!' including:

'Conventional profanity delays just can't compete with ARSE! and 'Simple on-screen controls, level meters and status information make ARSE! a dream to use!'

2 Live Crew Declared 'Obscene' Shock

In 1990 a Florida judge declared that the album *Nasty As They Wanna Be* from the rap group 2 Live Crew was legally obscene and that stockists faced possible criminal prosecution. His decision was soon ratified by Indiana, Ohio, Pennsylvania, Tennessee and Wisconsin. Just reading some of their song titles might have hinted at the verdict before the courts became involved in their lengthy legal investigations.

Baby Baby Please (Just A Little More Head)

Bad Ass Bitch

Bill So Horny

Dick Almighty

Dirty Nursery Rhymes

Face Down Ass Up

A Fuck Is A Fuck

The Fuck Shop

H-B-C (Head, Booty and Cock)

Me So Horny

P-A-N (Pussy Ass Nigga)

Pop That Pussy
Savage in The Sack
Ugly As Fuck
We Want Some Pussy
When We Get Them Hoes
Who's Fuckin' Who

N.B. In 1985 a part-time record clerk was arrested in Callaway, Florida, for selling a copy of 2 Live Crew's album *Is What We Are* to a fourteen-year-old boy. In one of the songs on the album the singer talks about his 'big black dick', which according to him, is 'fifteen inches long and eight inches thick'.

An Obscene Phone Call?

Callers to NTL's customer service helpline received a rude awakening recently. Instead of hearing the usual apologies about high call levels and waiting time, all they got was, 'We don't give a fuck about you basically, and we are not going to handle any of your complaints. Just fuck off and leave us alone'.

The message was changed by Ashley Gibbins of Redcar, Cleveland, who'd been kept on hold for more than an hour by NTL while trying to subscribe to their broadband service. He discovered by chance that he could remotely change the recorded message – and it was heard for two hours until NTL deleted it.

Police arrested Mr Gibbons and charged him under the Communications Act 2003 with making 'a grossly offensive message'. The case was thrown out by magistrates after they consulted Chambers dictionary and decided that while the word 'fuck' was offensive, it was not grossly offensive.

Rupert Everett on 'Fuck'

Actor Rupert Everett was quoted as saying, 'I don't mind bad words – for instance, fuck. I think it's amazing that it's a swear word. After all, it's something most everyone likes doing. It's sweet and harmless. We've overanalyzed things to make something pejorative out of an experience that's so nice. That's a weird madness.'

%$@#£&* Censors!

Reinhold Aman, a linguist from Santa Rosa, California, has spent 25 years collecting profanities that have appeared in the media. Since 1977, his results have been published in a series of books called *Maledicta* (Latin for 'bad words') and also in a quarterly newsletter, *Maledicta Monitor*, which has 1,500 subscribers.

Anything short of printing the full word incenses Aman, after all, he says, 'If you use f·ck, we all know what it means, so why should spelling it out in full make anyone more upset?'

These are some of the methods editors use to censor profanities:

1. Dropping vowels (e.g. f-ck, c*nt, sh*t).

2. Dropping all letters except the first (e.g. f---, s***).

3. Inserting the phrases [expletive deleted], [vulgarity deleted] or [blasphemy deleted].

4. Changing the word (e.g. changing 'hell' to 'heck', 'fuck' to 'fudge').

5. Substituting all the letters except the first with an underline (e.g. c____. Aman has said, 'There's a big difference between cocksucker and cunt.')

6. Inserting dingbats (e.g. $%@#!).

COMPETITION

After the copious research conducted for this book, we are still dissatisfied with the quality of swearing in the English language and feel that there is still great potential for real obscenity as yet untapped.

We are therefore launching a unique competition. We would like you to attempt to construct the rudest sentence ever composed in the English language (in not more than 35 words) and send it to:

Berkeley Hunt
Summersdale Publishers Ltd
46 West Street
Chichester
West Sussex
PO19 1RP
UK

Really Daft Ideas

D. I. Saster

£4.99 Pb

Some ideas should never have made it further than the half-witted minds they originated from. *Really Daft Ideas* picks out the pottiest true stories to make you laugh and cringe.

From the soldier who tied a hammock between two wall lockers, only to be fatally crushed by them at bedtime, to the man who took aim at a spider crawling up his leg and shot himself instead, this book demonstrates why it's a good idea to think before you act.

YOU KNOW YOU'RE A CHILD OF THE '80s WHEN...

Mark Leigh & Mike Lepine

£4.99 Hb

Flashdance... Kajagoogoo... Top Gun... Nik Kershaw... Transformers... The A-Team... Fraggle Rock... Knight Rider... pixie boots... Pac Man... Smurfs... Stock, Aitken and Waterman... Care Bears... body-popping... puffball skirts... Donkey Kong...

Do you remember these and are not afraid to admit it? If so, shake off your Reebok Hi-Tops, put on your Relax t-shirt, loosen your stone-washed jeans and see if you really are a true child of the '80s!

Mark Leigh and **Mike Lepine** have written humour books with Adrian Edmondson, Julian Clary, Jeremy Beadle, Roy Chubby Brown and Chris Tarrant.

THE LITTLE BOOK OF

ESSENTIAL FOREIGN INSULTS

Emma Burgess

£2.99 Pb

Communicating your superior opinions to Johnny Foreigner can be an uphill struggle at the best of times, but with this essential phrase book you can indulge in derogatory discourse wherever you travel and make sure they get the message.

THE LITTLE BOOK OF

ESSENTIAL ENGLISH SWEAR WORDS

Stewart Ferris

£2.99 Pb

Thicker, wider, longer-lasting – yes, you too can have a vocabulary that impresses your friends, family and prospective employers. The English language has a rich tradition of exquisite words, but you can forget about all that and just master the ones lying unloved in the literary gutter.

www.summersdale.com